DREAM AND WONDER

DREAM AND WONDER

A CHILD'S VIEW OF CANADIAN VILLAGE LIFE

Elsa Redekopp

Illustrated by Margaret Quiring

Kindred Press

Winnipeg, MB, Canada   Hillsboro, KS, U.S.A.

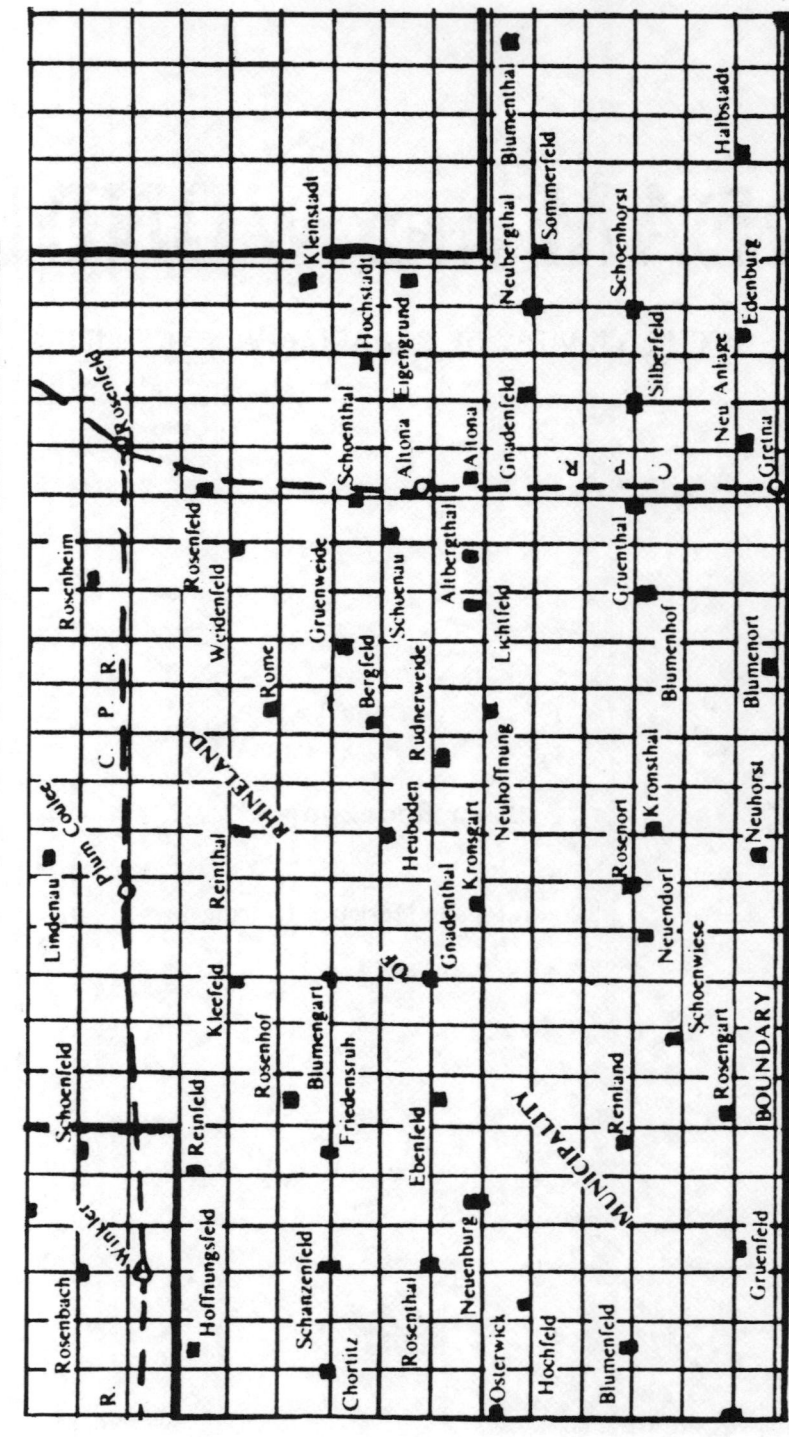

CONTENTS

The Violin Makers 1
The Crust of Bread 9
A Scare 13
A Strange Experience 16
The Contest 18
Going to Church 22
A Sunday Wedding 31
The Haybarn 37
A Faraway Friend 44
School 48
The Singing Lesson 52
Lisa Turns Teacher 56
Fall Butchering 61
Stories on the Ovenbench 67
The Skunk 73
Ma Comes to Canada 76
A Chalice for Christmas 80
Preparing for New Year's 87
Bringing in the New Year 91
New Year's Day 97
Valentine's Day Preparations 101
Easter 107
Egg Rolling 113
Music Lessons 116

Dream and Wonder

Copyright © 1986 by Elsa Redekopp, Winnipeg

All rights reserved with the exception of brief excerpts for reviews, no part of this book may be reproduced without the written permission of the publisher, Kindred Press.

Published simultaneously by Kindred Press, Winnipeg, R2L 2E5 and Kindred Press, Hillsboro, Kansas 67063.

Printed in Canada by the Christian Press, Winnipeg

Design by Gilbert G. Brandt

Illustrations by Margaret Quiring

International Standard Book Number   0-919797-44-X

Dedicated
To all the boys and girls
who requested another book about
Lisa

The Violin Makers

In the small village of Gnadenthal, set on the endless southern Manitoba prairie, two young boys were totally absorbed in a very special project. They were in the process of making a violin out of a piece of old lumber found in their father's workshop.

They had read that a long time ago in Italy, a man named Stradivarius carved beautiful violins by hand. These instruments became valuable and famous all over the world. Arn had seen the name "Stradivarius" printed inside a violin that Mr. Kuhl played at Music Night on Saturdays.

Ever since the musicians gathered at Lisa's house on Saturday nights, Arn had wished for a violin. He already played tunes on the violin Mr. Kuhl lent him from time to time. But Arn knew that if he ever expected to play in a group, he needed one of his own. Besides, somewhere he had read that to do well you must play every day. The thought of buying a violin was out of the question. Not even a whole summer of gopher hunting would bring enough money to pay for one.

Gerd, always helpful, said there was no problem, "We'll make a violin. All we need is a piece of lumber and an outline. You said Stradivarius made his own by hand, didn't you? Well, so can we. We have wood."

"Yes, but I think he used special wood that was

quite old and dry!"

"All the better," said Gerd. "Old wood we have plenty of. Here, look at this pile of boards."

"But the fingerboard is made of very hard black wood, and Stradivarius used a special varnish."

"We'll use black paint for the fingerboard; and Pa has some old cans of varnish. That should be special enough!"

"And will you put your name inside like Stradivarius did?" Lisa asked, full of curiosity "You can see his name through the f-holes in Mr. Kuhl's violin!"

Sitting on the wooden log nearby, Lisa observed the proceedings with keen interest. Arn and Gerd, used to Lisa trailing them, tolerated, conveniently ignored, or found her useful to run errands as the occasion required. Lisa had no objections and happily followed all their activities with admiration. All, except gopher hunting! This new project should prove to be exciting. Nobody in the village had ever made a violin before!

Arn finally paused to answer Lisa, "Oh, that name means that it is only a machine made copy, not hand-crafted. The real handmade ones are very, very expensive. If we sold our house and farm there would not be enough to pay for even one of them. Great artists like Heifetz and Kreisler play them in Europe and in cities like New York and Boston. The sound must be heavenly! I wonder if I'll ever hear a great violinist like that. But this is Manitoba, never mind Gnadenthal, in the middle of nowhere!"

With all her heart Lisa wished for Arn to hear a great artist someday!

Arn was telling Gerd that he had read of a Stradivarius that cost as much as $10,000. Lisa, awestruck, visualized a luminous shiny instrument.

"Was it made of gold, Arn," she asked wide-eyed.

"No, of course not, it was carved from wood as well. What makes these instruments so valuable is the special varnish Stradivarius used. It was a secret recipe that no one ever discovered or was able to imitate."

Lisa thought about the secret recipe as she wandered around the workshop. The long crude workbench bore marks and gouges where hammers, clamps and chisels had shaped household furnishings, at times even simple wooden toys. In one corner stood the cobbler's bench, much used to repair shoes, boots and harnesses. The walls were hung with the basic tools, hammers, pliers, saws and wrenches. But the heart of the workshop was the great iron anvil resting on a huge block of wood. Here Pa sharpened ploughshares, shaped horseshoes, fashioned metal containers and repaired broken machinery, sometimes causing sparks to fly from the hot metal. The smell of wood, leather and metal combined to give the room an aura all its own.

That night Arn traced the outline of Mr. Kuhl's violin on a large sheet of brown paper. Today, immediately after school, he placed the pattern on a smooth board that Gerd had chosen and marked the outline with Pa's big carpenter pencil. They needed two equal parts, one for the top and one for the back.

Using Pa's saw, Gerd worked around the outline. It was awkward to get around the curves with the big saw. With Pa's file, Arn carefully marked the spaces for the sound to come through. These were shaped like an f and were called f-holes.

"How will you cut those f-holes with your big saw?" Gerd paused to ask.

"That is a problem. It cannot be done without a special tool. If only Pa had a fret saw!"

Lisa wished that Jacob, her older brother, were here. He had answers for everything. But at sixteen Jacob already worked for a family in the village of Rosengart, to help pay for the farm.

Lisa saw Gerd's hand go up to pull his right ear. He always did that when he was thinking hard. She waited expectantly.

"Problem solved," he announced. "We can use the pocket knife I got for Christmas!"

After all, hadn't he fashioned arrows and whistles

and slingshots with it?

Each day after school, Lisa watched Gerd set to work. Meanwhile Arn used the chisel to gouge out the violin back to the right thickness. He planned also to use the chisel to carve the intricate scroll. Maybe he would make it in the shape of a lion's head or an eagle's. He chiselled faster at the thought of such possibilities. It would be the most unique violin in the village. And it would be his very own!

Pa walked in with a leather harness to be mended. Quietly he observed the activity. "So that's what you *Jungens* (young fellows) are doing. That wood is not easy to work with!"

"We used only scrap lumber, Pa. We cut out the top and back. Now we need to cut the neck. The bridge takes only a small piece but it has to be very strong to support the strings. The sound holes are the problem, Pa!"

"Yes, I see," Pa nodded, quietly watching Gerd labor over the fancy shape with his pocketknife. Shaking his head, he slowly walked back to the house. Following Pa, Lisa wondered why he did not seem to share the excitement of the boy's project.

Mother slid the last batch of golden brown *zwieback* off the hot pan, adding to the mound already on the bright oilcloth-covered table. The aroma of baking and freshly brewed coffee filled the large kitchen.

Ma went back to her buttermaking. Pushing the dasher up and down in the barrel-shaped churn was tiring work. Sometimes it took very long for the cream to turn to butter. Finally Ma lifted the lid. Lisa could see the creamy lumps floating in the buttermilk, some clinging to the sides. Scooping some from the edge with her finger, Lisa tasted. It was so good she felt like eating gobs of the rich smooth butter.

"Here, Lisa, I'll scoop some into a saucer for your *zwieback*. Later I will strain the rest and put it in buttermolds. I know it always tastes best fresh from the churn," Ma laughed, setting the saucer on the table.

Pulling a *zwieback* apart, Lisa smoothed the creamy

spread over the fluffy inside. She could not think of anything that might taste better!

"I'm ready for *fesper*," Ma sighed as she poured freshly brewed coffee and pulled out a chair.

Lost in thought, Pa took a sip from his steaming cup and reached for a *zwieback*.

"Mother, something has to be done. For days now Gerd and Arn have spent their spare time making a violin, using saw and pocketknife. Little do they know the complications even with the proper tools. They still have not faced the problems with the soundpost, never mind the pegs."

Ma listened, for the moment too tired to respond. She could not think of a solution.

"Something has to be done," Pa repeated. "We must think of a way to get a violin."

Lisa listened intently, sure that Ma would pronounce such an idea impossible. There simply never was enough money, not even for shoes.

To Lisa's surprise Ma said, after a while, "I am thinking about the egg money. If the hens lay well we could perhaps save enough to order a violin from the Eaton's catalogue. I have seen a violin priced at $5.00. That is costly, but it includes the bow and case and extra strings. And if our Jersey cow freshens, we might get some extra butter money."

Ma and Pa discussed the possibilities. Five dollars was a lot of money. Eggs were only five cents a dozen and the only cash income for the large family. It would take time to save that much.

Ma looked at Pa's patched work boots, realizing how badly he needed new ones. He repaired and resoled the family shoes in his workshop, but he did not have the tools to make new ones.

"I can always add another one," Pa laughed, studying the variegated shades of leather patches already there. Ma also laughed at the sight, then sighed. "Well, I suppose we must get the fiddle." She looked around at the bare windows. Her secret wish for frilly curtains would have to wait again.

"But what about the rule we made, Father? No extras, only barest necessities until the Immigration Debt is repaid to the C.P.R. Company!"

Lisa felt a sudden chill. There it was again, the invisible monster, the Debt that loomed over the family, causing Ma and Pa so much concern.

"Perhaps, Mother, we will have to consider this a necessity," Pa replied firmly.

"Yes, I suppose we must. The boys will be too discouraged when it does not work, after trying so hard," Ma remarked, scraping bits of butter from the upturned lid of the churn.

"Ma," Lisa broke in, "Arn says the proper name for a fiddle is a violin. I'll tell the boys right away!"

"Wait, wait! In our discussion I forgot that you were listening, owl! Let's not tell for a while! After all, we must try to save enough money first. My little owl can keep a secret, can't she?" Pa teased, fondly rumpling Lisa's hair.

This was even better. Lisa loved secrets and immediately wanted to share it with someone. Just then Leni ran in, flushed and breathless. She and her friend Irma had played in the haybarn. As Leni hungrily bit into a crusty *zwieback,* Lisa was about to tell her. But she had promised. Besides Leni was too young to keep a secret. Instead, she would run and tell Irma right away. No, she would not tell, except perhaps her very dearest friend, Lili.

She thought about it as she watched Ma strain the lumps of butter, leaving the buttermilk stored in an earthen crock. Cold buttermilk made a refreshing drink and also was good for baking. With a small wooden paddle Ma worked the creamy lump over and over in a bowl of cold water, until the water was completely clear. She added a little salt to the butter, mixing thoroughly. Now Ma rinsed the buttermold. The oblong form held exactly one pound of butter. Ma filled the mold tightly, smoothing the top evenly with the wooden paddle. The bottom of the mold was decorated with long carved grooves. Ma turned it upside down over a plate and pushed the handle attached to the bottom of the buttermold. Lisa and Leni watched intently. Out came a cream-colored, perfect pound of butter with a handsome design on top. Usually there was enough for Ma to make three pounds of butter.

While she watched, Lisa felt a prickle of delight whenever she thought of the violin in the Eaton's catalogue.

The Crust of Bread

Looking around the supper table Lisa observed everyone eating heartily while listening to the brothers' animated discussion of their latest gopher hunt.

Ma's fluffy bread, spread with chokecherry jam, was delicious, leaving purple traces on Lisa's face. She loved Ma's good bread, but the crusts were hard and crumbly. Quickly she pushed her crust under the edge of the plate. Ma was very strict about eating everything on the plate, even crusts. Later Lisa intended to take the crust to Rover, the family dog, who would love the treat.

Nobody noticed, except Gerd. He never talked much, but very little escaped him. He followed Lisa through the kitchen door that led to the barn.

"Come Lisa, I'll give you a push on the swing," he offered.

Pa had tied a long heavy rope to the high rafters of the haybarn to make a swing. The swing was so high that it was hard to start without a good push. Lisa settled herself on the wooden seat and grasped the rope on either side. Gerd started her gently.

"About that crust, Lisa, you know the rules. Perhaps you don't understand why Ma cannot bear to see any food wasted. She thinks of the time in Russia when a crust was a matter of life or death.

"I was six years old when all our crops and gardens

were destroyed by the communist regime. They said everything belonged to them. They stole all our chickens, cows and horses. There was nothing left to eat. Every night we all went to bed without food and woke up so very hungry in the morning.

"For a while we children all cried and begged for bread, but Ma had nothing to give us. I remember how we hunted for food, something to eat, anything. One day we found some sunflower seeds behind a board in the wall. Jacob climbed trees looking for crow's eggs to eat. We wanted to dig for roots but it was too early in the spring. The ground was still too frozen.

"One day Arn found a treasure under the porch— an old red beet, all shrivelled up. Trembling with excitement he ran to show Ma. With the beet Ma cooked some soup and we all had hot broth. Then we had nothing to eat for many days. We grew weaker everyday, until we could hardly get up in the morning. Schools were closed because the children were too feeble to attend.

"With tears in her eyes Ma would plead with us, *'Kinder, geht doch draussen spielen im Sonnenschein!'* (Children, go out into the sunshine to play).

"But we could not play. We were too weak from hunger. We did not even cry any more. And that is why Ma cannot bear to see us waste food, even crusts. The memory of that time is too painful."

The swing came to a stop. Lisa had listened intently. She shivered, suddenly feeling cold. So it was not only the crust, it was much more. She looked at Gerd, big blue eyes wide with concern.

"But Gerd what happened? When you almost died, did you get food again?"

"That is the good part Lisa. We were all dying. But just at that time the Mennonite Central Committee came to our rescue. They were a group of concerned people from Canada and the United States who sent flour, rice and sugar. Big kitchens were set up where food was prepared. Once a day all the children could go for food. How anxiously we waited and watched the clock all morning. At eleven o'clock we ran to stand in line, holding our tin cups. Each child received a tall narrow pan-bun and a cup of cocoa. We were not allowed to take food home, we had to eat it right there. Very often Jacob and I drank our cocoa but ate only half the bun. We hid the other half in our pockets to take home. Then Ma and Pa could eat too, because they had nothing at all.''

Lisa was very quiet on the swing. After a while she said, "That is such a sad story; but it was a happy ending because now we all have enough to eat! But I wish that nobody in the whole world would ever be as hungry as you were.''

"Wishing is not enough Lisa. We have to help as much as we can.'' Gerd gave the swing a gentle push as he left to finish chores.

Lisa wondered how she could possibly help. There was no money. How could she send food to faraway places? Suddenly she brightened. Of course, why hadn't she though of it before.

The picture of the Good Shepherd carrying the little lost lamb safely through the wilderness flashed through her mind. She would tell him all about it. Surely he would also care about all the children in the world.

With a burst of relief she started pumping the swing, going higher and higher. The rush of air reddened her cheeks, making her long hair stream out behind her. It was a wonderful day after all. And even crusts were good!

A Scare

One spring morning Lisa watched Ma mix a big batter of honey cake. This was a family standby. There was always a large pan of it on the pantry shelf. Lili and Irma sometimes stopped by after school for a piece of honey cake.

"This cake should really be made with watermelon syrup. In Russia we had big fields of watermelon and we made our own syrup. That homemade syrup gave the cake a special flavor. But honey is good too, although it makes a heavier cake," Ma explained, scraping the batter into a large pan. Lisa picked up the spoon to lick it.

"It's almost better before it's baked, Ma. Do you think I could learn to make it?"

Smiling, Ma nodded and showed her the recipe. It was in German, written in Grandma's thin spidery Gothic script. But Lisa could read it and found the recipe fairly simple.

Syrup Cake
1 cup butter
2 cups honey (or thin syrup)
2 eggs
4 cups flour
1 cup buttermilk
2 tsp soda
1 tsp spice

Heat the oven with straw till the bricks glow white. Put your hand in the oven and count to seven. If it starts to burn your hand the oven is ready. Put the cake on the oven rack and bake for half an hour.

The last instruction looked rather complicated, Lisa thought, as she watched Ma test the brick oven and put in the cake.

"Should I go to the back garden and see if the rhubarb is up yet?" Lisa asked reaching for her coat behind the door.

"Be sure to cover your ears well. These spring days are chilly and we don't want any earaches!"

Lisa pulled the red woollen toque over her ears. It was a Christmas present from Tante Anna. The toque was bright and warm. Lisa walked across the yard still filled with puddles from the spring thaw. Some puddles were lightly frozen over with silvery spears of ice. It was fun to crunch these with her rubber boots as she walked to the granary. The great garden lay directly behind this building and in this sheltered spot the rhubarb sometimes appeared quite early.

All over the yard the chickens were busily scratching and pecking for seeds and worms. What silly, harmless creatures they were! Lisa called Rover but he did not appear. He must have gone to the fields with Gerd she thought, as she continued by herself.

Suddenly, a savage creature pounced on her from behind with a fury that threw her down on her face, knocking the breath out of her! She felt sharp claws through her coat and a strong beating of wings. Something was fiercely pecking her head. She screamed in terror, unable to move! The creature held her down digging its claws into her.

Arn came dashing out of the barn with a big broom in his hands. Furiously he whacked the great red rooster till he fell off. The rooster staggered and tumbled around dizzily from the hard blow.

"Ma, Ma, come quick! I've killed the rooster!" Arn

cried in anguish over his violent attack. He knew how valuable the rooster was.

Ma hurried out. "Quick, get the axe Arn!"

She pulled the rooster over to the chopping block near the summer house. With a quick blow of the sharp axe, she chopped off his head. The rooster stopped flapping, then lay still. Arn felt terrible.

"He would have died anyway, children. This way he did not suffer," Ma explained. "Besides, it is time we had a good chicken soup!"

Lisa was still shaking and trembling. The great red rooster had terrified her, yet she still felt sorry for him. Why had he attacked her?

"Roosters are very protective of their hens. Red means danger. When the rooster saw your red toque he wanted to protect his hens from an enemy," Arn explained.

That night they had chicken soup for supper. It was always a favorite, especially the fine homemade egg noodles. Ma rolled out the paper-thin pastry, then cut it into long strips. She layered these strips and with swift strokes cut them into fine threads. The soup smelled wonderful but Lisa, remembering the afternoon's events, did not feel like eating any.

Later, at bedtime, Lisa still shivered from the shock.

"The rooster could have killed you and then you would be dead," Leni said, contemplating such interesting possibilities. "You would lie in the coffin in a white dress. Your hands would be folded, holding flowers and we would all cry and say how good you were!"

Already moved by the sadness of the scene, Lisa suddenly realized, "But I couldn't see any of it if I were dead. Anyway, Arn saved my life. He is a hero, just like David or Samson . . . or . . . Robin Hood." She was casting about in her mind for more suitable examples.

"And I never did find out whether the rhubarb was up!"

A Strange Experience

The Friday spelling match was a good ending for the week. Lisa and Lili sometimes were opponents, each the leader of a team. In the end the spelling match sometimes turned out to be an endurance test. One time neither could spell the other down and the match was tied. Lisa enjoyed spelling because the words were fascinating, especially long ones like "hallucination" or "chlorophyll."

During Lisa's year in Grade IV, Mr. Schaefer made an important announcement. The Department of Education had sent out a general spelling test to be given to all the students from Grade IV to X in all the schools in the province. This sounded very important. Sheets of paper were handed out. Lisa was glad she had just started Grade IV because now she could be in the spelling test too. It would probably be very hard if it were a test for Grade X also. Never before had all the classes from Grade IV up written the same test.

When they were ready, Mr. Schaefer dictated the words from the Department sheet, repeating each word very slowly and clearly. Some words were hard but most of them were easy, and Lisa settled down to enjoy the test right to the end.

Lisa was disappointed when she found out that she had made one mistake. She had spelled "all right" as one word "alright." Mr. Schaefer asked all those to stand who had fifty words correct or more. Lisa stood with many others as he called out for those with sixty or more. At eighty or more the Grade X's were still standing. At ninety and more, Lisa turned and found she was standing alone. Even the Grade X's were down. She felt strange and embarrassed and quickly sat down. "Your mark is 98%, you had one mistake, Lisa. All right is two words," Mr. Schaefer said with an encouraging smile. Everyone looked at her. She felt strangely uncomfortable. It was almost like being different. She was worried the big boys would not like it. But at recess Sam and John said, "Good for you, Lisa, you beat us all!"

At supper that night, Pa said, "Look what our owl did today! 98% on a Department test and she's only in Grade IV. Who knows where all this will end?"

Lisa did not mind Pa's teasing. But the whole thing made her feel uncomfortable. After all it had been so easy.

It was not until much later that Lisa realized what a fine teacher she had.

Pa came home from a School Board meeting one day to announce that the Department of Education was bringing out-of-province educators to her school. The Gnadenthal school was chosen because the students' writing in English was well above the Manitoba average even though English was their second language.

Pa said that the School Board was very pleased but surprised because each school day was so demanding on the children: 8:30 German language instruction, 9:00-3:30 Departmental requirements in English, 3:30-4:00 Religious instruction, and 4:00-4:30 instruction in German literature. Besides, all this was taught by one teacher to eight grades with an enrolment of over forty students. Pa said that the officials wanted to see first-hand how a teacher could achieve such high educational standards with such a heavy curriculum.

Lisa never thought that the school day was long. She wished it were longer so that there would be less time for chores.

The Contest

The arrival of the Free Press Prairie Farmer in Lisa's home was a weekly highlight. It usually arrived on Saturday. Lisa spread the comic section out on the freshly scrubbed kitchen floor and asked Arn to read Little Orphan Annie with her. She was grateful for his unfailing patience. Together they followed Annie's adventures with her faithful dog, Sandy.

Once in school, Lisa had soon learned to read the comics by herself. Then Arn taught her to do the weekly crossword puzzles. Trying to match new words across and down became an exciting game. Sometimes Lisa found the right word before Arn did, but she didn't know that he let her.

But the best part of the Free Press was the Junior Club section which had letters from all parts of Canada. Many of these letters asked for pen pals to share hobbies and interests. Sometimes the section featured a game, puzzle or short story.

One Saturday there was a special announcement. With great interest Lisa read "Junior Club Story Contest" offering first, second and third prizes.

Lisa liked telling stories but she wondered if she could write one good enough for a contest. She would think about that. She enjoyed writing compositions for school but she always had to wait for the glow inside. Sometimes it took a long time but when she felt the glow it spread all over her with the joy to write. Lisa's mind buzzed with ideas during the next days. When the glow came, she decided to write a wishing story about a boy named Tom who wanted a guitar more than anything in the world. But she would not tell anyone because she felt very shy about trying something so unusual.

Lisa found that the story came quite easily. But she wrote it over and over many times on brown paper before she felt it was right. Then she copied it very carefully on white lined paper. While she addressed the envelope to the Junior Club she wondered about the stamp. Sometimes there were none in the house. Pa had none, but Jacob said he would take it along to Plum Coulee to buy a stamp and mail it there. Lisa was greatly relieved. Jacob always found ways and means, often by virtue of gopher tails.

"Who is your letter for, owl?" Pa asked, surprised at this unusual activity.

"It is for Junior Club, but it is a secret, Pa," she said timidly.

"If secrets make you happy, have all you want, owl," Pa remarked, returning to his paper, "as long as you don't ask for too many stamps. We cannot trade eggs at the post office, you know!"

Lisa was relieved that no one asked her further about the letter. She felt too shy about telling anyone, except Lili, her best friend. With Lili she shared almost everything.

Only yesterday she called Lili over to see what Arn had brought home from his hike to the field pasture. Under the willowbush near the creek he found a clump of crocuses. They were a pale mauve color with a soft yellow centre. When Lisa touched the petals they felt like soft furry velvet. Lili picked up a crocus.

"Do they smell nice?"

"Oh, Lili, don't! You must never smell a crocus! Arn says smelling a crocus makes your nose swell up something awful."

Quickly Lili backed away at this dreadful warning. All of Arn's pronouncements were received by the girls as gospel truth.

Later in spring Arn came home from his field excursion with a pail of creek water. Carefully he emptied the contents into a big glass sealer. Through the glass they could see a mass of white transparent globs stuck together. It looked like a lump of white tapioca pudding.

"These are frog's eggs," Arn announced to the girls with grand authority. "These will turn into live frogs in a few weeks' time."

"Frogs in a jar?" Lisa shuddered.

"See the black dot in each egg? That will grow into a tadpole with a little tail. Then it will grow legs, drop the tail and end up as a real frog!" With this statement he instructed Lisa and Lili to watch the jar carefully each day. The black dots grew larger and larger until one day almost overnight they saw tiny tadpoles darting around in the water. They called for Arn.

"Come quick! They are alive!"

"Of course they are alive, I told you so," Arn stated loftily, taking complete credit for this transformation. Their respect for Arn increased considerably once more.

Soon tiny legs appeared. The tadpole tail was gone and behold there was a tiny baby frog, perfect in every way. And to think that it grew in a jar!

Warm summer rain brought its own pleasures for the girls. After a heavy downpour, the grassy ditches on either side of the street were overflowing. When the sun came out, cries of delight rang from one end of the village to the other. Children of all ages waded and splashed in the warm clean water. Lisa and Lili joined Leni and Irma to revel in the warm water with the cool green grass underneath.

Little boys and girls sometimes lost their balance coming up gasping and sputtering with shrieks of joy. Laughing mothers held the hands of the smallest ones, guiding them along the shallow edge of the ditch. For once not worrying about clean clothes, they let the children splash and play to their heart's content.

Even Mrs. Janzen, in spite of her strict code of cleanliness, allowed herself to smile indulgently at the spectacle. Mothers laughed and chatted and for a moment forgot the everlasting chores and tasks.

"Look, look, a rainbow!" Leni shouted, pointing up. There it was far above the tall poplars in all its gentle shades against the deep blue sky.

"It's the promise," Lisa heard the mothers say softly.

Going to Church

The wonderful fragrance of freshly brewed coffee alone made Sunday a special day. On weekdays roasted barley called *"prips"* was served. Pa said it was much healthier, but it lacked the aroma that spoke of an unattainable world of luxury and leisure.

After the Scripture reading, Lisa and Leni recited grace in unison very carefully. If said too quickly, they might have to repeat it again.

Pulling apart a golden buttery *zwieback*, Lisa spread the tangy chokecherry jelly over the fluffy inside. Leni already had a purple mustache. Pointing at her, Lisa said, "Your mouth is purple," and giggled. Both broke into helpless laughter and couldn't stop. Ma started laughing too.

Trying to restore order, Pa said, "Children, at the table you should talk about sensible things!"

Composing themselves, Lisa and Leni finished their *zwieback*. With a quick *danke* (thank you) to Ma, they ran out the back door into the flower garden to find the hummingbirds.

Every house in the village had a large flower garden facing the street. This garden was separated from the sidewalk by a board fence extending the length of the village, flanked by a row of tall Manitoba maples and poplars. Lisa loved these trees. She liked to put her arms around them feeling the rough bark against her cheeks, enjoying the woody smell and the solidity of the old trunk. The trees had given, and always would give, a feeling of security and a sense of foreverness.

All four gardens, including the huge vegetable field, the two cherry ones and the front garden, were kept immaculately hoed and raked. But the flower garden was the pride and joy of every home, tended with love and care. The path running from the back porch to the street was trimmed and swept every Saturday. The sunlit garden was filled with flowers of every description in prim, orderly rows. The center was bordered by a big circle of green chives sprouting purple blooms. Inside this border grew a profusion of red and white sweet williams, purple pansies, yellow nasturtiums and pink phlox. Along the fence, like troops on parade, were tiger lilies proudly flaunting their showy orange blooms. Lisa felt a little shy about them; the tiger lilies seemed so bold. Flanking the side fence were the gentler morning glories in soft pinks and blues.

But the special ones were the *morgenblumen* (four-o-clocks) planted in a straight row along the path close to the house. The lowly leafy bushes opened their bright red blooms only at sunrise and at sunset. The girls tiptoed down the prim row.

"There they are, two of them!" Lisa whispered.

With a faint humming of wings in constant motion, like miniature propellors, the tiny birds hovered over bushes, then dipped their long beaks deep into the heart of the red blossoms drinking in the sweet nectar. Leni always hoped to catch one to see what it looked like when the wings were still. Lisa thought of them as magical creatures, maybe from fairyland. Perhaps they were sent to fetch nectar for the Fairy Queen.

"Come quickly, look what I found!" Leni called, forgetting to whisper.

There, hidden in the leafy stems under the flowers, was the tiniest brown nest, no bigger than a walnut.

"Don't touch, Leni," Lisa whispered. "Arn says that birds never return if their nest is touched!"

They observed the brown little nest with awe,

wondering if there might be eggs in it.

"Let's show it to Arn," Leni said.

Just then Ma called. "Come children, it's time for church. Leni, I will braid your hair while Lisa gets dressed, then I'll do hers."

As they walked down the road to the little gray church, Lisa looked back. Pa, in his Sunday suit looked even bigger than usual, reminding Lisa of the sturdy maple trees, strong and secure. Ma, as usual, wore her best black dress. It was one of the few things Ma had been able to bring from Europe.

The rich black satin moire with puffed sleeves and heavy black lace applique over the front ended in a high stand-up collar to frame her face. In this dress Ma, her rich brown hair gathered up, looked like a queen. Lisa liked the rustle of the stiff satin skirt as they walked. On Sundays, Ma wore a black satin bow on top of her hair. It was a tradition for a new bride to wear a white bow but later this was replaced by the black bow worn for special occasions.

Ma and the girls settled down on the straight wooden bench on the women's side. When the girls were smaller, Ma used to form her white hankie into the shape of a doll, a frog, or rabbit for them to play with. Now they only needed to be reminded to keep their feet still and not to whisper to the children in front of them. Ma exchanged smiles and nods with the ladies around. The church filled up quickly. Behind them sat Mrs. Janzen, smiling benignly, confident certain matters were known to her alone. She was the village midwife, the mainstay in times of illness or events connected with illness. Mrs. Janzen was considered an almost omnipotent deity whose authority was unquestioned when consulted on all matters relating to physical frailties.

Not only did she dispense her medical skills where needed, but many times she carried in her medicine bag a jug of hearty chicken soup for a new mother or a needy family. The village children believed that she carried babies in her black medicine bag and placed

them wherever she pleased. Lisa blushed remembering how she asked Mrs. Janzen to please bring a baby for a gift to Margaret's wedding. But that was when she was five years old!

Her kind round face always looked scrubbed and polished like a rosy apple. Even her glasses sparkled. A faint antiseptic odor emanated from her as though she had been freshly starched and sterilized. At the arrival of a new baby, Mrs. Janzen took over the entire household, ordering, admonishing, and regulating affairs to the common good of all concerned. Her authority was unquestioned and undisputed. Even Mr. Hein, the village tough, feared for his temper by all, meekly obeyed her strict instructions to scrub thoroughly before entering the sickroom. The village was gently ruled by Mrs. Janzen who felt commissioned to impose her standards of hygiene on everyone.

It had been said that her teenage niece, Hattie, secretly demonstrated her defiance of this reign of cleanliness. A friend was a witness to one occasion where Hattie set the table for supper in preparation for her aunt's return from a sick call. With her bare big toe, she carefully circled each dinner plate before setting it on the snowy white tablecloth. No one was ever the wiser, but when Lisa heard about it she often wondered what might have happened had anyone found out!

Three rows back, Mrs. Penner nodded a cheerful greeting. Lisa liked Mrs. Penner with her harmless interest in one and all. Next to her sat Mrs. Krohn, the hardest worker of the village, who seemed to accomplish more than anyone else. Her house and yard were more immaculate, if such were possible, than any other, heaping unspoken guilt on said villagers. Six days a week she outworked one and all. On the seventh day, with house, barn and yard in perfect order, she rested. Like God, Lisa thought.

Mrs. Krohn was also most generous and befriended many a destitute immigrant family that arrived. Lisa remembered, when they moved in, how Mrs. Krohn had sent over a box of clothes her children had outgrown. There was an especially pretty pink dress that was just Leni's size. Lisa had been more than a little envious.

But to Lisa the fascinating part about Mrs. Krohn was her golden earrings. She wore gold hoops that went right through her earlobes and she wore them everyday. The only gold Lisa had ever seen was Ma's narrow wedding band and Mr. Penner's golden tooth. Mrs. Krohn's golden hoops filled her with an aura of royalty, bringing kings and queens to mind.

Lisa wished Ma could have gold earrings. Just then a shaft of morning sun stole in through the tall church window. It touched Ma's hair, turning it red-gold against the black satin bow. Yes, Ma looked elegant even without the gold earrings!

The congregation started the first verse of *"Nun danket alle Gott"* (Now thank we all our God). Ma did not open her hymn book because she knew most of the songs from memory. Lisa knew them too. Singing very quietly, she listened to the clear sopranos and altos harmonizing with the strong lower voices on the men's side. It was a rich and noble sound like waves of harmony swelling to the very rafters.

There was a general rustling as the congregation rose for prayer. Looking down, Lisa observed the shoes along the row, brown or black, mostly worn and scuffed under the careful polishing. Only Lili and Ella had new shiny shoes. Ma said if the hens laid well this summer, Lisa might get a new pair with the egg money. Lisa was puzzled about that. Was not the egg money being saved for a violin? Had Ma forgotten about the boys' need for a violin? The boys had struggled so hard to make a violin, but so far nothing had worked right. A violin would be such a good thing. Of course, new shoes would make her feel special. She wondered whether it was all right to pray for the hens to lay well, when she was startled by a strong "Amen!"

204

Nr. 189. BM 85.

D-dur, a=5.   Martin Luther, 1483—1546.

Ein fe = ste Burg ist un = ser Gott, ein gu = te
er hilft uns frei aus al = ler Not, die uns jetzt

Wehr und Waf = fen;
hat be = trof = fen. Der alt bö = se Feind mit

Ernst ers jetzt meint; groß Macht und viel List sein

grau = sam Rü = stung ist, auf Erd ist nicht seins = glei = chen.

Martin Luther, 1483—1546.

As the congregation settled down, the choir rose to sing. Lisa leaned back to listen. The conductor raised a tuning fork to his ear and hummed the opening chord giving the correct pitch to the singers. The choir sang from a sheet with printed numbers, called *ziffern* (or numbers) instead of notes. It was a very, very old form of music.

Reverend Bueckert based his sermon on the text of Psalm 23. Lisa could already recite it. She studied her Sunday School picture of the Good Shepherd carrying the little lost lamb on his shoulder. Just to look at it made her feel safe and secure.

Lisa's eyes wandered to the great oak beams supporting the ceiling. Pa had explained that the beams served a special purpose. The first settlers in Gnadenthal had worked very hard raising enough food for their families. Sometimes crops failed because of drought, hail or grasshoppers. Continually, new settlers came in who needed help. The village council decided that each farmer would set aside an amount of grain to be stored in the church attic. When a family was in need, they could receive relief to tide them over. Nobody in the village need go hungry. It was a good way of helping one another. Pa called it the Village Welfare System. Lisa wondered whether there was still grain up in the attic.

"And so my beloved, may the blessing of the Lord go with you," the Reverend Bueckert intoned in his gentle Sunday voice.

Lisa wondered about the blessing. How long did the blessing last? Could you keep it? Was it just for now, or forever, or did it get used up? She felt a blessing whenever she looked at the picture of the Good Shepherd. Perhaps the blessing would always come back whenever she looked at it again.

Outside, she joined the circle of girls making plans for the afternoon. Mrs. Penner stopped Ma to inquire about those absent. Was Mrs. Wiebe down with her migraine again? Where was the Peters family? Ma thought they might have gone to visit relatives in

Reinland, and would attend church there. What about the Funk family at the far end of the village? Heads were shaken in concern. Things did not seem to be going too well there. Was it perhaps a matter of illness? All eyes turned to Mrs. Janzen who, smiling benignly, was not about to divulge any information known to her alone.

Ma and the ladies agreed that a big pot of chicken soup for the Funk family could do no harm.

A Sunday Wedding

Wedding news was the exciting topic at lunch this Sunday. Lunch consisted of chilled fruit soup, cold sliced ham, and potato salad made the day before. Sunday was to be a day of rest, but the afternoon wedding would change all that.

After the dishes were done, Lisa and Leni were free to play until the wedding began. Lisa climbed up to her favorite perch, the board fence facing the street. It made a fine grandstand from which to observe all passing activities. She called to Lili across the street.

"Come Lili, let's walk the fence!"

For a while they tried balancing carefully. Lili was small and agile and kept walking a long time without falling off. Lili was also the fastest runner in school. Only Nettie could keep up with her.

Lili almost lost her balance as she noticed the approaching cloud of dust. A rider on a proud horse came galloping down the street. It was young Jack who practically lived on his handsome horse. He rode by with a great flourish, making his horse rear dangerously to impress the girls. They stared in awe, wondering where he was off to. Most likely to the Hutterite village for a fox hunt. Jack was always daring, always on the edge of adventure or mischief, inviting either admiration or punishment. For mischief he certainly held the record. The girls eyed him with secret admiration, covered up with virtuous disdain.

"I think Jack likes you, Lisa!" Lili teased.

"Never," retorted Lisa, startled at the thought.

"Yes, he does," teased Lili impishly.

Lisa quickly pointed down to the path. "Look, the choir girls are coming early to practice for the wedding."

In the distance they saw the flutter of summery dresses. Lisa admired the young ladies greatly; they were so lovely and graceful. One lady whom she particularly admired was Tina, who lived across the street with Susie. Tina, tall and slender, wore her long blond hair gathered in a soft coil. One day when Lisa played at Susie's house, Tina had brushed out her hair. It was the golden color of a ripened wheat field and was so long that she could sit on it. Lisa looked at her own thick braids. They were a mousy color and not nearly as long. Remembering, Lisa sighed.

"Someday I would like to be as beautiful as Tina, and as nice. She always stops to talk to us. Even when I was only in Kindergarten, she sometimes stopped me on the way home to ask me to sing the new songs I had learned. I felt really important to sing for her. She specially liked this one from Hansel and Gretel:

>   Brüderlein komm tanz mit mir
>   Beide Hände reich ich Dir
>   Einmal hin, einmal her
>   Ringsherum das ist nicht schwer!

Lili joined in the actions. Both girls ended the song in much laughter.

"Anne is nice too. I like her brown curly hair and her pretty face," Lili said.

"And you know Lili, I think my brother Gerd likes Anne. I've seen Gerd walk her home from church on Sunday evenings. I wonder if they will sit together at the wedding today?" Lisa wondered.

There was much on which to speculate. Today was the wedding of Frank and Sanna. Frank was already recognized by the congregation as a young, gifted speaker. Sanna, a black-haired, brown-eyed beauty, was considered a perfect match for him.

The wedding letter had made the rounds from house to house listing the names of the invited guests. Lisa and Lili were glad their families were on the list. In the end, nobody was left out. It would be a big wedding for all to enjoy.

The church filled up quickly. Lisa and Lili chose seats up front close to the aisle, so as not to miss anything. They needed all possible information pertinent to their paper doll wedding ceremonies. After all, weddings were not exactly alike. They could always use new ideas to add variety to their paper doll ceremonies.

A hush settled on the congregation. At the conductor's signal, the choir rose to sing a traditional greeting, *Gott Grusse Euch* (God Greet You). It was such an old song that the music was still in *ziffern* (numbers) instead of notes. All heads turned to watch the bridal couple start slowly down the aisle, Frank tall and handsome in a navy blue suit, Sanna radiant, her brown eyes shining through the shimmering veil fastened to her black hair with sprigs of green myrtle. She seemed to proceed in a filmy cloud as she slowly moved forward on Frank's arm to the waiting chairs in front. All through the meditation and the ceremony, Lisa could not take her eyes off the bride. As they knelt for the blessing, a shaft of sun gently touched the silky sheen of her hair through the veil like a gentle benediction. Lisa felt a stab of joy almost like pain at the beauty of the moment.

The choir sang *Auf Adler's Flügeln* (On the Wings of an Eagle), a profoundly moving song about shelter and safety under the wings of an eagle through life's storms. Then the bridal couple walked out to the congregational song, *Jesu, geh Voran* (Jesus, Lead the Way).

Chattering and laughing, the guests made their way to the big red granary at the bride's home. The wooden floor had been scrubbed spotless. Long tables with white tablecloths and dishes collected from the

whole neighborhood had been set the day before. Each table was decorated with a jar of bright garden flowers. The walls and beams overhead were covered with leafy green branches, giving a lacy bower effect.

Platters of golden *zwieback,* bowls of sugar cubes and dill pickles were set out. The young men in snowy white shirts made the rounds, pouring coffee, while the girls in their summery dresses refilled the plates as they were emptied. There was milk for the children, but Lisa and Lili had coffee just like the grownups, with *zwieback* and sugar cubes to be dipped. The little boys at the next table ate with bulging cheeks, then stuffed their pockets with sugar cubes and ran out to play.

Lisa and Lili made very sure not to miss any part of the program that followed later that night. There were humorous recitations, a short meditation, and some amusing anecdotes about the young couple. The choir rendered songs in a lighter vein like *Lindenbaum, Still Ruht der See, Waldesruh.* Lisa and Lili made note of these songs for their next paper doll wedding.

Best of all was the orchestra. Lisa never got tired of it, the violins, guitars, and mandolins joining in the full rich throbbing sound.

Now the young ladies surrounded the bride for the customary removal of the veil and wreath. In its place a white satin bow was fastened to the bride's hair, symbolic of her new status as a young wife. The veil was put on a plate held by the bride who was now blindfolded. The young ladies then formed a circle around her and sang their traditional wedding song.

Blindfolded, the bride walked around the circle, holding out the plate to the nearest girl who was then considered to become the next bride. The young man who received the groom's boutonniere was to be the next groom. Anne, blushing furiously, received the veil and Gerd happened to get the boutonniere!

The young men now lifted Frank and Sanna on chairs up high in the air to kiss, which they did very gladly. Then Anne and Gerd had to sit on chairs to be lifted up for kissing. Every time the crowd chanted "Sweeten life with a kiss," they had to kiss. Gerd for once forgot his shyness, and made full use of a golden opportunity. Again and again they were lifted high, surrounded by applause, until the young men were satisfied.

The wedding activities now moved outdoors to the big green yard. Forming a large circle, the young people started their game of *Schlüsselbund* (Keyring). Jacob started singing *Hab oft im Kreise der Lieben* (Often in the Circle of Love) as he went up to choose Tina for his partner. The young men all chose partners as they continued to sing and move forward. Jacob had started singing *Du, du liegst mir im Herzen* (You, You are on my Heart) when he threw his bunch of keys into the center. The signal was a rush to exchange partners. The last person to do so had to pick up the keys and start the game with a new song. The evening continued with a variety of singing games.

In the gentle light of the summer moon, the girls, flitting around in their filmy dresses, long hair tied in colorful bows, created a fairy-like scene. The snowy-white shirts and lusty singing of the young men added an extra touch of romance.

Lisa and Lili, sitting on the sidelines, followed the changing of partners with greatest interest. Someday they too would be part of that wonderful world of weddings and games.

The Haybarn

The chores of cooking, cleaning and washing for a large family were endless. Ma needed all the help she could get. Lisa and Leni picked vegetables, peeled potatoes, set tables and washed the never-ending dishes.

But after lunch there was a space of free time. While Leni ran over to play with Irma, Lisa escaped to her favorite hideout. She clutched a book, climbed up the steep ladder of the great haybarn and pulled herself up on the rough dusty floorboard of the hayloft. Making a cozy hollow in the new hay, she curled up with her book. In this fragrant nest she could read and dream to her heart's content. Sometimes she just listened to the soothing patter of the raindrops on the roof above, drinking in the sweet scent of the new hay that spoke of green meadows and fields of clover.

She could watch a spider hang from a dusty rafter by an unseen thread, or hear the chirping of a cricket in a far corner. She listened to the gentle cooing of the pigeons on the roof and the swish of the swift swallows in and out of their nest under the eaves.

The swallows were her favorites, their flight full of grace and dartlike precision like streaks of delight. They seemed so joyous, so sure, so free! They did not sing, but the elegance of their flight, their flash in the sun like the sheen of blueblack polished steel, gave her a profound rush of joy.

Or was it pain? She could not define it. As with the song of the meadowlark, the pain was to reach out and capture the beauty to hold forever but being unable to do so. She could only hug herself trying to keep the feeling and wait for the next moment. She knew the feeling would leave but she also knew that it would come back at unexpected times without warning. It was something nobody could take away from her. A lovely secret not to be shared because it could not be put into words.

She loved these little nooks of time in the busy summer afternoons. Here she spent hours with Heidi of the Alps, gloried in the adventures of Robin Hood, cried her way through Oliver Twist, grieved at the death of Beth in Little Women.

Lisa had felt the anguish and the triumph of Judah Ben Hur and wanted desperately to share the story with Ma. But Ma did not understand English too well. Lisa decided to translate chapter by chapter. As Ma sat on the wide front porch mending the family garments, Lisa read and translated Ben Hur into German. She wanted to draw Ma into the magic of ancient Jerusalem, the hills of Judea, the Roman chariots, the galley slaves and the lepers. How could she convey the joy of the healing miracle and the wonderful reunion of mother, sister and brother? It was a slow painstaking task, but Ma had listened patiently through the summer afternoons.

Here in the hayloft Lisa could enjoy her collection of dreams stored away in her mind. It used to be a collection of wishes but wishing was different from wanting. Wishing was unlimited and need not necessarily come true. Wanting and not getting sometimes hurt, like wanting a box of paints or a bicycle. Her wishes had changed into a treasury of dreams, to take out and enjoy one by one. And best of all, she had a friend and kindred spirit, Lili, to share them in this secret place.

Together they read, talked and planned in their

fragrant sanctuary. They discussed books, artists, and royalty. Some day they would go to Europe and each fall in love with a prince and live in his castle forever and have all the things they ever wished for. Fantasy made everything possible.

"Lili, what would you like to be some day?" Lisa asked, sitting up to arrange a bigger bunch of hay for her pillow.

"Oh I think I will be a teacher like my father. I would read many stories to my class and give them very little arithmetic!"

"I would like to be a painter, Lili, and draw people and paint beautiful sunsets. I would love to paint a Madonna like Raphael. But you must have talent, Pa says. What is talent, Lili? How long does it last? And does it get used up if you keep on painting? Must you save talent so it does not run out like food or money?"

Lili thought about that and found no explanation, but she would ask her father. He always had answers.

"One thing I know for sure, Lili. I don't want to marry and be a mother. Mothers never play, they only work. Ma has hardly any time to read, so sometimes I read to her while she works. Even on Sundays Ma never rests, especially when company comes. Sometimes she is too tired to even go to church on Sunday. That reminds me, I promised Ma I'd bring straw to heat the bakeoven for her bread. I must call Leni to help carry."

"No Lisa, I'll help you carry the straw basket!" Lili offered.

Ignoring the ladder, the girls jumped down into the high mound of hay below, disappearing into the softness with giggles of delight. At the far end of the haybarn they heaped the great willow basket with clean yellow straw.

"Lili, have you heard from your pen pal in Junior Club? Isn't it exciting to write to someone far away that you might never see? Perhaps she will send you a picture. I would like a pen pal but it is a matter of stamps. Lili, I have a secret. Promise not to tell?"

Lili solemnly promised, hand over heart.

"It's a secret because I feel strange about it. I sent in a story for the Junior Club Competition several weeks ago. Jacob mailed it for me in Plum Coulee. If I get a prize, I would have my own money for stamps."

Lili viewed Lisa with awe: "You did? Oh, Lisa, I'm sure you'll win, your stories are always so good. When will you know?"

"Maybe never! I have waited for a long time now. You see Lili, this is wanting and wanting is different from wishing. I really want that prize money very badly! Then I could get stamps and have a pen pal too! But I think my story was not good enough because I would have heard by now. Every day I have watched for the post man but nothing has happened. So please don't tell anyone I even tried!"

Lili had no answer. Quietly they grabbed a handle at either end of the huge basket to carry it to the bakeoven behind the summer house. They were careful not to spill any across the neatly raked front yard.

Wearing a wide brimmed straw hat, Ma had already started the fire. She was stirring the embers with a long-handled iron fork as she waited for more straw to feed the oven.

"You came just in time girls. Set it down here. Lisa, the post man came just now. He brought the *Bote* and the *Abendschule* and something for you, a letter and a package. Whatever could it be, and where did it come from?"

Ma picked it up from the garden bench and handed it over. Lisa held the brown paper parcel, stunned and speechless. Never before in all her eleven years had she received mail, not even one letter of her very own. But here was her name on the parcel clearly typed, not written. It was unbelievable! She hoped she wouldn't wake up and find it just a dream.

"Open it, open it, Lisa!" Lili urged impatiently,

hopping from foot to foot.

With unsteady fingers Lisa managed to unwrap the package. She opened a small gift box. In it lay a shiny bracelet sparkling like gold. Her heart skipped a beat. She had never seen anything so beautiful. It was breathtaking!

"Lisa, it's the prize money for your story from Junior Club," Lili cried, hopping around harder than ever. "Here, open the letter, hurry!"

Shakily Lisa read the letter. Her story, Tom's Wish, had won first prize in the Junior Club Story Contest.

Lili read over Lisa's shoulder, "It says, 'Congratulations!' What does that mean? And look what's in the envelope!"

Lili pulled out a crisp green dollar bill, brand new. It was prize money!

Lisa stood motionless, unable to fully accept such sudden joy. She listened as Lili translated the letter over again for Ma. She explained to Ma about the contest. Ma smiled, shaking her head at such an amazing and wonderful occurrence.

Lisa could barely hold so much happiness. If only she could keep this moment forever. It all came together, the meadowlark, the sunsets, the music, the Madonna and now this wonderful moment.

And what would Pa say? He would be pleased, take her on his knee and say, "Whatever will we do with this little owl!"

A Faraway Friend

Lisa tingled with excitement at the very thought of the trip. They were going to visit Friesens in Sommerfeld. Because the long drive could not be made in one day, they would have to stay overnight. Lisa loved the thought of this visit to her faraway friend, Marie.

Marie's father owned Pa's farm. After each harvest season Pa drove to Mr. Friesen to pay the rent. This time Lisa's joy about the trip was tinged with sadness as she watched Pa's anxious face as he went about his chores. From bits of conversation she understood that there was not enough money to cover the rent. The field and garden crops had been very poor for lack of rain. Lisa had heard that some villagers lost their farms when they could not pay the rent. She felt a sudden chill at the thought of it. How terrible to lose the farm when Pa had worked such long hard hours from dawn to dusk.

She tried to tell herself that Mr. Friesen was always so kind and helpful, surely he would understand. Going to the cherry garden, Lisa firmly pushed these thoughts aside. She wanted to bring a gift to her faraway friend, Marie. Pincherries did not grow in Sommerfeld. Marie loved them so Lisa picked enough of the shiny red cherries to fill a whole shoebox.

Early next morning Ma packed lunch in a large cardboard box. She put in buttery *zwieback,* some smoked sausage, boiled eggs, tomatoes, dill pickles, a jar of coffee and one of water. Arn hitched the horses to the buggy. Lisa and Leni climbed on top of the wooden box behind Ma and Pa's seat. Arn settled down on a bale of hay on the buggy floor.

With a light slap of the reins, Pa started the horses down the driveway to the street. As Lisa and Leni waved to Anni, sitting on the wooden fence, they felt sorry for her and all those who were not going to Sommerfeld today. Overcome with the excitement of this wonderful adventure, the girls hugged each other.

Soon the village disappeared in the distance as fields of green and gold went by. For miles there was not a house in sight, only black-eyed Susans nodding from the grassy ditches, and distant trees indicating another village. The hot summer sun beat down as the soft dry dust rose, stirred up by the buggy wheels. Flies swarmed around the horses in droves. Now Leni realized what horses' tails were for. They went swish, swish to shoo off the swarms of flies. Arn felt sorry for the horses. When Pa let them slow down to a walk Arn jumped off the buggy to walk with them. He picked tall weeds from the grassy ditch and shooed off the flies where the horses' tails could not reach.

As it grew hotter, Lisa became very thirsty and tired, but she did not want to fuss. Just as she wondered about lunch, Pa stopped the horses at a clump of poplar trees by the roadside. They all climbed down and relaxed under the cool shade of the tall trees. Ma opened the box. Boiled eggs, tomatoes and dill pickles never tasted so good! And Ma had added a surprise treat—gooseberry turnovers! It was a wonderful picnic. As Arn led the horses to the nearby creek, Lisa watched them reach down and drink and drink. After that the horses enjoyed nibbling the thick green grass on the bank. Leni was glad that the horses had a picnic too. Anxiously, Lisa looked over at Pa. His face seemed relaxed. Ma hummed as she busied herself with the lunch.

As she watched Ma, Lisa wondered why mothers never played. The neverending tasks of cooking, washing and mending left no time. Ma was content to just relax quietly whenever she had a brief space of time. Lisa decided that she would never be a mother. Mothers never played, they only worked.

There was still a long way to go to Sommerfeld. After a while Lisa dozed off when suddenly the buggy stopped. They had arrived at Friesens. Her legs felt so numb and stiff she could hardly move. As Pa lifted her down, Marie came running out of the house to greet them. The girls looked at each other and laughed. Soon they were all in the house being welcomed by Mrs. Friesen. She had a round rosy face that was always smiling.

Ma felt shy about arriving unexpectedly at supper time but Mrs. Friesen assured her that there was plenty. Something smelled very good. The wonderful aroma of smoked sausage and onions slowly frying made Lisa very hungry.

Mr. Friesen came in to wash up from chores, beaming broadly as he welcomed the visitors. Lisa noticed that he too had a round ruddy face, always smiling warmly just like Mrs. Friesen. At the table, Marie sat between Lisa and Leni chattering happily. Mrs. Friesen served a heaping bowl of homemade noodles to go with the smoked sausage and fried onions in cream gravy. Lisa giggled when she saw Marie put chokecherry jam on her noodles. She tried some too. It was very good. She had learned something new from her friend! Marie had the bluest sparkling eyes and a round rosy smiling face just like her mother. It was good to know such a nice family!

After supper Marie took the girls to her room. All the floors, including her room, were covered with shiny linoleum, not like the plain wooden floors at home. Marie had a wonderful Eaton's Beauty doll with long real curls, whose eyes could open and shut, and a little baby doll with a tiny lace cap and gown. Marie let Lisa and Leni hold the dolls. Marie took out her little tea set and they spent the evening playing house. In one corner of the room Lisa noticed a bunch of big round balls in colors of pink and red and blue. They seemed to float in the air. Marie said they were balloons and took one down for her. It was light as air and floated around the room.

Now Mrs. Friesen called the children to the living room to get ready for bed. She had arranged quilts on the floor for the girls. What fun to sleep on the floor together!

Mr. Friesen and Pa had talked all evening. The anxious look had left Pa's face and Lisa felt that Mr. Friesen had worked things out again. Mr. Friesen's kind blue eyes twinkled as he asked Lisa for a song. She remembered his treats from the past. She felt a little shy because she was older now. Still for him she gladly sang his favorite 'Hansel and Gretel' song. Mr. Friesen smiled more than ever as his hand came out of his pocket with a shiny penny for each of the girls.

Just then Lisa remembered to give Marie the shoebox. Marie was delighted with the bright red pincherries.

"Thank you Lisa and Leni, I love pincherries and they do not grow here. I have something for you too. Tomorrow we will go into the bush to pick *Mehlbeeren* (miniberries). I know you like them and they do not grow in Gnadenthal."

Soon the girls were snuggled down on the quilts on the floor. In the darkness they whispered for a long time about the plans for the next day.

It was like being in another country, Lisa thought drowsily.

School

Lisa quietly put down her pencil on the arithmetic scribbler. She was done! Now she could turn and listen to Mr. Schaefer's history lesson with the Grade IX class at the back. Mr. Schaefer must be the most wonderful teacher in the world. He seemed to know much more than the history contained in the book. Kings and queens and conquerors became real and alive!

Today he continued the story of Napoleon marching through Europe to Russia. Although they had already read it, the class listened enthralled to the slowly unfolding drama of Napoleon's defeat. Lisa absorbed it all and stored it away as a special treasure. She would tell Pa all about it at suppertime.

Mr. Schaefer continued with a literature class. The class was studying "The Lady of Shalott" by Tennyson. The words flowed like a musical murmuring:

>On either side the river lie
>Green fields of barley and of rye
>That clothe the world and meet the sky
>And through the field the road runs by
>The Lady of Shalott.

For a moment she glanced at Lili beside her, deeply absorbed in Grimm's Fairy Tales. Lisa felt a stab of joy in having a friend who loved books as much as she did. It must be wonderful to have a teacher for a

father, someone who could answer any question that came to mind.

Sighing with contentment, Lisa again turned her attention to the classes at the back of the room. There were Nelly and Hanna, model students who could recite their assigned poetry flawlessly. At the very back sat Sam and John who always worked silently because they were correspondence students. They were held in awe and respect by the entire classroom.

Up closer was a group all its own, Jack, Dave and David.

Dave always sat with his cousin Jack. This combination was watched with interest by one and all since it was predictably unpredictable. During the course of the day some unusual activity could be expected from their location. Any untoward happening naturally made these two suspect.

One time a distinct smell of smoke wafted to the front. Dave and Jack were studiously bent over their history books, yet it certainly emanated from that area. No evidence could be found since the extinguished matches were safely hidden in their leather boots. Jack's face was actually cherubic as he turned unblinking innocent eyes on the class. Yet everyone knew. Lisa and Lili with the other girls, properly shocked by such bad behavior, felt all the more virtuous for it. At other times, old rubber rings found their targets across the room, usually undetected. Other pocket treasures were sunflower seeds, pieces of string, carefully hoarded cigarette butts and the odd gopher tail, a highly valued trade-in. An intermittent scuffling of feet was evident, the foot work serving as a secret code for messages or warnings. Jack's blue eyes could meet a teacher's with the unblinking stare of total innocence while delivering a vicious pinch to his desk partner by way of a friendly gesture. And he managed to get by without homework.

One morning Mr. Schaefer, asked the Grade VII class for the short essay assigned a week ago to be read orally. The first one to be called was Jack who never had any intention of writing it. Everyone knew that of course. With great assurance he rose, picked up his brand new scribbler, opened it to the first blank page and started to read his essay, "The Fox."

"The fox is a wild animal that lives on the open prairie. He is very smart and survives by hunting smaller animals, like rabbits and mice. His fur is very valuable and hunters . . . ."

He could have pulled it off. However, seeing the blank page, the boys behind him could not contain themselves any longer. A snicker, then another, gave the show away. Mr. Schaefer, pleased at first with the unexpected fluency, picked up the scribbler in a flash.

"This will be dealt with after school," was the message, heavy with portent. Lisa and Lili whispered about the dire consequences of such cheating. It was quite shocking behavior they solemnly agreed.

Again Lisa sat entranced listening to Mr. Schaefer's flow of poetry at the back of the room.

> And the night shall be filled with music
> And the cares that infest the day
> Shall fold their tents like the Arabs
> And silently steal away. (Longfellow)

It was something to remember and keep forever. Nobody could take it away.

During the reading, Mr. Schaefer walked up and down the aisle. While turning his back, Jack and Dave made faces at the girls across the aisle, crossing their eyes to make them laugh. Clearly, the boys did not succumb to the beauty of Longfellow's poetry. For them it was more important to make the most of the here and now to survive the system.

All day Lisa waited for the last half hour, the German literature period. Mr. Schaefer seemed to have an inexhaustible treasury of German poems and stories. For several days the senior class had studied *'Die Glocke'* by Schiller. Each episode was exciting as the drama of the great bell unfolded verse by verse.

The Singing Lesson

Lisa could hardly wait for next Friday. Mr. Schaefer had announced a singing lesson for that afternoon.

Lisa wondered how Mr. Schaefer could teach a song when everyone knew that he could not carry a tune. This was quite evident when he joined the class in "O Canada." But the villagers one and all agreed that he was such a wonderful teacher that this did not matter at all.

He knew a great deal about music and Lisa listened eagerly when he taught the upper grades about great composers like Handel and Haydn. But still, how would he teach songs, Lisa wondered.

Perhaps Mrs. Schaefer would teach singing. She was a wonderful singer and pianist and hers was the only piano in the village. On summer evenings the villagers stopped by to listen to the sounds of Bach and Beethoven floating through the open windows of the teacherage. But Mrs. Schaefer had two little boys to take care of and the school was a mile away from her home.

Today Mr. Schaefer tried his singing plan. He chose Nelly and Hanna, two of the older girls, to go to his home during the lunch hour. Here Mrs. Schaefer drilled a song with the girls until they knew the melody. Hurrying back to school they sang it over and over. Meanwhile the entire classroom, beginners and up, waited in suspense. Nelly and Hanna arrived quite breathless and sang as best they could. After a while the students joined in, repeating it several times. Mr. Schaefer had the children sing the song every day of the week until the next Friday when a new song was taught. The entire school of fifty students learned a new song each week in this fashion.

It was a good way to learn songs, Lisa thought. Many a tune was literally carried along the village road to the schoolhouse. The villagers tending house and garden smiled as they caught snatches of song drifting by. They were pleased at having such a fine caring teacher. Their children came home with "Sweet Afton," "Billy Boy," "Aura Lee," and of course the wonderful collection of German folksongs.

Lisa and Lili sang heartily, eager to learn new melodies. Mr. Schaefer, so anxious to have a school choir, was pleased with the eager participation with, of course, one exception. The boys, Jack and Dave, sat in sullen silence, refusing to join in. They had agreed that singing was beneath them and to be taught by girls their age was especially unacceptable. When admonished, they insisted they could not sing a single note.

Mr. Schaefer exhorted and finally commanded. They obliged! Into the lovely melody of "Evening Bells" broke an incessant droning which continued throughout the song to the distress of all.

As Mr. Schaefer walked along the aisle solicitously bending down to discern the sound, they droned louder in a continuous monotone. Shaking his head sadly he gave up. "*Sonderbar, sonderbar* (strange, strange)," he murmured. Clearly the case was hopeless. The boys could not carry a tune. They were therefore left alone during this period.

Lisa and Lili were frustrated with such behavior. First of all the boys pretended to be tone deaf and then they spoiled the lovely song with their dreadful droning. It was horrible. The girls discussed their behavior, savoring the delicious dreadfulness. They decided never to talk to these boys anymore. It would serve them right if they never got any girl friends. No girl in her right mind would want to be seen with such terrible characters. Some day they would be sorry.

The classroom was separated from the cloakroom by a partial half wall extending across the room. This half wall was a favorite perch for the boys before the teacher's return from lunch. Jack especially made this his grandstand for great orations.

On this particular day a sudden rain stopped the outdoor activities at noon. As the children took cover in the classroom, Jack swung himself up on the half wall to entertain them. With exaggerated gestures he described the fox-hunt in which he had taken part in the nearby Hutterite village. He became more and more excited, featuring himself and his horse as the heroes of the adventure. Not wanting to stop at the end of his story he suddenly burst into song:

"Do you ken John Peele
With his coat so gay
Do you ken John Peele
At the break of day
Do you ken John Peeeeeeeele
When he's far far away---

He stopped in mid-song. All the hubbub ceased and an alarming silence descended. All faces turned to the door. There stood Mr. Schaefer, returning unexpectedly early. Jack slid off the wall trying to disappear among the students.

But the truth was out. Jack could sing and sing well. Mr. Schaefer took off his coat with an amused expression on his face.

"Good afternoon boys and girls! Well, well, well, what have we here, a singing lesson. I know you can hardly wait Jack, but we will continue with an hour of singing after recess!"

There was no more droning during song sessions.

Lisa Turns Teacher

Lisa loved school. To miss even one day of school would have seemed tragic for her.

Everyday she came home with interesting things to tell Ma. Her teacher knew absolutely everything; you could ask about anything in the whole world. Today for instance, Mr. Schaefer had discussed ancient Greece with the Grade X class at the back of the room. It seemed as though he had been there himself. Helen of Troy, Perseus and Achilles came alive. Instead of doing her Grade V work, Lisa had tried to visualize Helen of Troy, the most beautiful woman in the world; how lovely she must have been, fair of face with hair of gold. Enthusiastically Lisa had listened to the story of the Wooden Horse and the capture of Troy.

Stirring the bean soup bubbling in the iron pot, Ma laughed as she listened.

"Remember your first day of school Lisa? You took a pile of textbooks, including the big geography, expecting to read them right away. How disappointed you were when you came home. You had not used any of them!"

Lisa still blushed when she remembered that! Yes, she had expected to read those books the very first day. She thought going to school would be like magic. The teacher would wave a wand, like the good fairy, and instantly the children would read.

"I was terribly disappointed Ma, but I liked school anyway. I could sit with my best friend and draw and color and listen to other classes. And we did learn new words everyday."

"The men will be in for supper soon. Better take care of the lamps Lisa, and then set the table."

Lamps were Lisa's job. She went for some old newspapers, careful to choose only farm reports. The other pages might be interesting to read again. The lamps were lined up on the shelf beside the brick oven. Lifting the glass cylinder, she pushed the crumpled paper in, twisting and turning till all the smoky film rubbed off. Removing the soiled paper she used another to polish both the inside and outside until the glass was clear and shiny.

Yes, she remembered that first day of school, especially not reading instantly. But she also remembered exactly when she discovered she could read. It was always fun to learn words like cat, bat and rat, that Mr. Schaefer printed on the board. But those were just words. Would she ever learn to read like her brothers could?

One evening she paged through Arn's brown reader, looking for her most favorite picture again, 'The Madonna of the Chair.' She loved the gentle face of the mother and child, the lovely hands, the rich folds of drapery, even though the picture was only in black and white.

She went on to the next page and looked at the words, "A-fisherman-and-his-wife-lived-in-a-hut-by-the-sea." She was reading! She read on and on. She could read!

"Pa, look, look I can read!" she cried, and started to read the story out loud to him. Pa was very proud.

"Oh, Pa, I read the whole story. I can read the whole book!"

Lisa could hardly stop reading. She read every book in sight. Now Arn would not have to read to her anymore. She would read Little Orphan Annie all by herself. She would read all her brother's books. And everytime, it was like opening a magic door to a whole new world, unlimited and endless!

Till now Ma had always led her into storyland with Frau Holle, Hansel and Gretel and the story of Genoveva. Genoveva always brought tears to Ma's eyes, it was so sad. Perhaps now Lisa could tell stories to Ma in return.

After supper the lamp was lit and all gathered around the kitchen table. Ma was mending clothes, the boys were doing homework. Pa often read out loud from books of Fritz Reuter and Schiller, his favorite German writers. Sometimes he read Tolstoy or Dostoyevsky in Russian which only Ma could understand. Lisa and Leni giggled at the strange sound of the Russian words.

"The Russian language is one of the most poetic and expressive, children," Pa explained patiently. "But listen, I will read a beautiful German poem by Goethe that you will understand."

It was lovely, and Lisa was glad she could understand the German language. Pa read Russian and German so well, but he still could not read English.

"Pa since I can read I will teach you too! Here let's start right now!"

I'm too old to learn, owl," Pa laughed.

Ignoring his protests, Lisa settled down firmly beside him with her reader.

"Look Pa, it's easy. Let's try this verse."

Pa read, "Hey Deeddli, Deeddli
  The cat and the feeddli
  The cow yumped over the moon."

"No, no Pa, this is the way to say it," Lisa proceeded to read correctly.

  "Hey diddle diddle
  The cat and the fiddle
  The cow jumped over the moon."

"But owl, its not written that way, there is an 'e' at the end of fiddle. In German and Russian you pronounce every letter!"

Lisa realized she would have some problems with

this pupil. She would have to be very firm.

"Well, Pa, this is the right way. My teacher said so!"

And that was that.

Every evening after supper Lisa worked with Pa, sometimes only after much coaxing. Soon he could read the story of the Three Bears very well. Although Lisa was pleased with Pa, she still giggled at his pronunciations.

During these evenings Ma sometimes made a little treat. She stirred together two cups of brown sugar and two thirds cup milk to simmer on the stove. Then she added a lump of butter and vanilla, mixing well to pour into a pan to cool.

Every once in a while Leni would stop coloring to look at the big old Kroeger clock ticking away on the wall. She often wished it would go faster; but it simply went its own steady pace ignoring her impatience. The clock seemed to regulate the entire family, telling them when to eat, when to sleep, when to work.

Now the hand on the colorfully decorated face of the clock pointed to eight. Leni shut her coloring book. It was time for the treat! Everyone stopped working, including Pa, who was greatly relieved at a reprieve from his tireless tutor.

The rich chewy squares on the platter disappeared quickly. The rare treat made the evening special.

Now that Pa could read English, Lisa decided it was time to teach him arithmetic. Although he had been a fairly obedient pupil, he now put his foot down. Arithmetic was the same in German and Russian as well as in English.

And that was that!

Fall Butchering

Lisa woke with a start to find herself sitting up in bed. It was a sharp crack that woke her. Now she remembered, it was butchering day.

Ma and Pa had spent the day before preparing for this event. Ma baked and cooked and collected containers to hold meat, lard and cracklings. Pa built a fire under the huge iron kettle so the water would be at the boiling point by the morning.

Early this cold November morning, Pa's friends came to help, bringing their big sharp butcher knives. After the pig was killed, it was scalded in boiling water, and scraped to remove the bristles. Then it was hung from a beam in the hay barn and the insides put into a tub. While the carcass cooled, the men went in for breakfast.

Since it was very early and still dark, they ate by lamplight. Eagerly they drank the strong hot coffee. Thick slices of buttered bread disappeared with steaming bowls of porridge. Warmed and refreshed, Pa and the men went back to work. They cut hams, ribs, and huge pieces for roasts. There was liver to chop for liver sausage and headmeat for headcheese. The smaller bits of meat were collected in a tub to make sausages.

Now the women, shawled and aproned, arrived to help Ma. Mrs. Penner and Mrs. Dyck were efficient at making sausage casings. They took the tub of innards behind the barn to empty the intestines. They poured scalding water through the casings from the kettle spout. Turning the casings inside out they scraped them with knitting needles, till the casings became thin and transparent. Again they were thoroughly rinsed and boiled and sterilized, ready for the sausage machine.

During this time, the men ground the lean meat. Mr. Peter Penner was considered the expert sausage maker and he made a ceremony of his job. Rolling up his sleeves he scrubbed hands and arms. Then he set to work. Adding a handful of salt, a shake of pepper and spices, he set to mixing the big batch with great vigor, pausing ever so often to taste, shake his head and add more of this and that. At a chosen time he paused to look around for effect. He took a taste, closed his eyes for a long moment of suspense, then pronounced the mixture perfect.

Now the fun part began. Lisa and Leni watched the sausage making with fascination. The sterilized casings were stripped over the mouth of the sausage machine. Slowly the mixture was forced into the casings and tied up at the ends. These long sausages were hung in the smokehouse to be cured.

The other sausages, made from the chopped liver and spices, were short and fat. They were cooked in the huge outdoor kettle of bubbling fat. Mr. Janzen used a long wooden paddle to stir them until well done. After the liver sausages were lifted out, thick slabs of spareribs were lowered into the bubbling fat. These were cooked till most of the adhering fat was fried away and the lean meaty ribs remained to be eaten cold with homemade mustard.

In the end, all scraps of fat and meat were cooked in the great outdoor kettle. Mr. Janzen, with his wooden paddle, stirred and stirred, watching the fire carefully. Ma came over to skim out the bits of meat that had turned into crisp brown crackles.

The left-over fat was strained into large tin pails forming pure white lard. The light brown residue left

in the kettle was carefully collected. It was a flavorful nutritious spread good on brown bread, serving as a butter substitute.

Everything was used up. The pig's feet were scraped and cleaned and pickled. The head meat was chopped and seasoned and mixed with a hot broth. When cooled in the pan it came out in a nice jellied loaf ready to be sliced and eaten with vinegar and onions. Lisa and Leni did not care for it, but Pa and the boys liked headcheese for an evening snack.

Even the pig's stomach was scraped and scalded, to be filled with ground meat heavily spiced with garlic. This was the only time Ma ever used garlic. Then it was sewed up and hung in the smokehouse together with the hams and sausages. It acquired a wonderful smoky flavor suggestive of spices and garlic; a wonderful treat for a cold winter night.

By supper time all were weary and hungry. It was a well-earned reward to sit down at the table. Lisa had cleaned the lamp chimneys till they sparkled and then had set the table. Supper on this occasion was always the same; fresh liverwurst, cold spareribs with homemade mustard, fried potatoes and plenty of dill pickles, green tomato relish, and pickled watermelon. With the coffee, Ma served her special honey cake and peppermint cookies.

A leisurely discussion continued as to the number of hams and sausages in the smokehouse, the pails of lard rendered, the amount of spareribs and liverwurst stored in the cool pantry. The Penners asked Ma and Pa to their butchering next week Thursday. It was considered an honor to be invited for such an occasion.

The men retired to the *Grosse Stube* (Parlor) to sit on the ovenbench that ran along the brick oven. It was a restful time to discuss crops, village matters and the school situation. Pa was a trustee on the school board.

Ma and the ladies gathered up the dishes and the children helped to carry the food to the pantry. As they worked and chatted, the kitchen became neat and tidy again.

Ma and the ladies gathered in the *Kleine Stube* (like a family room) welcoming the cozy comfort of the brick oven against their backs as they chatted about the day's events and the next butchering at Penners.

The teacher and his family were always special guests at these occasions. Lili and Irma had brought their paper dolls and spread them out on the large kitchen table. Lisa had a whole shoebox of paper dolls that she had cut out of the old Eaton's catalogue. It was a large family and she kept adding to it as the occasion demanded. In case of a wedding, a groom was easily supplied from the men's wear section. He might be missing a leg or an arm cut off due to overlapping of other displays. But imagination made them all perfect and beautiful. They all had names and lived in the shoebox from day to day patiently awaiting such special occasions.

There was one set of paper people that lived from chapter to chapter of "Little Women." Meg, Jo, Beth, Amy and Laurie played their storybook parts whenever called upon. Poor Beth's death was the occasion of a very elaborate and emotional funeral giving scope to much crying and grieving.

Some of the paper population were named after movie stars whose pictures Lisa and Lili had seen in the newspaper. Beautiful Loretta Young, all unbeknown to her, had a huge family of children, including twins and triplets. Shirley Temple would have been amazed at all her brothers and sisters displayed on the kitchen table. An evening of much visiting and celebrating with paper people now began.

The gentle murmur of the ladies on the ovenbench drifted to the kitchen table and the world of paper dolls. Someone started a song which slowly tapered off. All were too tired to sing. Outside gusts of autumn wind rattled the shutters. But in this little world the Kroeger clock ticked away and all was safe and well.

As goodbyes were said, Ma thanked them all for their help. Pa held the oil lamp at the open door to light the path. The dim light of the lamp followed the departing guests like a gentle benediction.

Stories on the Ovenbench

"What was it like when you first came to Canada, Pa?" Lisa asked one cold wintry evening.

A blustery wind rattled the window shutters, heaping high snowdrifts around the house. Against the grey twilight Lisa could see the little white hills of snow nestling in the corner of each square window pane. With a tingle of joy it reminded her that Christmas was coming.

Inside all was warm and cosy. The steady ticking of the old Kroeger clock could be heard above the usual household noises. Pa just finished heating the great brick oven that extended to all the rooms of the house. It took three huge baskets of straw to feed it. When the flames died down the embers turned the inside into a crimson cave with the iron rack glowing red hot.

Ma shoved in the long black baking pan holding seven loaves of high risen dough and firmly shut the heavy door. The hot oven always reminded Lisa of the wicked witch in Hansel and Gretel who baked her gingerbread children.

In the next room a backless wooden ovenbench ran the full length of the brick oven. Above it was an iron side-door opening into the hollow brick top of the oven that served as a slow cooker. Here Ma set great pots of soup or stew to simmer all day. Tonight the rich fragrance of beans and sausage gently bubbling

in a rich broth, slowly spread through the whole house. Sitting on the ovenbench between Ma and Pa, Lisa and Leni felt very cosy. As she leaned against the whitewashed oven wall, Lisa enjoyed the warmth on her back as it slowly spread comfort through all of her being. Jacob, Gerd and Arn sat on the floor with a bowl of sunflower seeds between them. The seeds tasted good and were very healthy too, but Lisa had never quite mastered the knack of cracking the shell with her teeth like the boys could. Instead, she opened each laboriously with her fingers. By using this method she made little progress.

Lisa nudged Pa gently, repeating her question.

"What was it like when I came to Canada, owl? Then I must start from the beginning," Pa finally replied.

"Many years ago, our ancestors lived in West Germany. They were excellent farmers and good citizens and had a good life there. But they became very worried when a new king wanted to take away their religious freedom. At that time Catherine the Great of Russia sent a special invitation to the Mennonites to settle on, and cultivate, the great grass steppes of the Ukraine. In return she promised them freedom to worship and the right to keep their German language and build their own schools. Above all, they would never have to take up arms, for they honored God's commandment: 'Thou shalt not kill.'

"The Mennonites followed Queen Catherine's invitation to settle in her country and over the years turned the wild steppes into beautiful orchards and rich grain farms. Their Mennonite settlement became known as the 'breadbasket of Russia.' They built model villages with schools, churches, hospitals and beautiful gardens. It was a good life.

"Then the revolution came and everything was destroyed. The breadbasket was turned into a wasteland. Communist soldiers robbed, killed and burned whole villages. They took everything away from us saying it all belonged to the new government.

We nearly starved to death. Our only solution was to leave Russia. Just before this decision, our little baby boy, Ernest, died. After we buried him we left our home forever."

Pa was quiet for a while. He seemed to be far away in another time and place.

"Why did you choose to come to Canada?" Lisa inquired.

"Again it was because of an invitation, this time from the Canadian Pacific Railway Company. This company wanted settlers along their railways across the prairies. They offered to pay our voyage to Canada. However, we were to repay the loan plus interest within a certain time."

"I remember the ship," Gerd interrupted. "It was called the *Bruton*. It was an old cargo ship that was to be junked. But the C.P.R. officials said, 'Oh, just load it up with Mennonites. Because they pray a lot the ship will be sure to make the voyage!'"

"Well, it almost didn't make it," Jacob said. "While we were crossing the North Sea a great storm came up. The wind and waves were so fierce that the ship's wheel broke. I remember the terrible fear and excitement aboard. The crew desperately tried to repair the damage. I remember how Pa helped the crew with the ship's wheel."

"Yes Jacob, with all our manpower and heavy ropes we managed to hold the wheel together, so the *Bruton* finally made it to Southhampton, England.

"Here all immigrants had to undergo a health inspection. We were all cleared except Ma whose eyes suffered because of malnutrition. So Ma and baby Lisa were sent back to Germany. For a whole year they had to stay in the old army barracks of Lager Lechfeld. Now after the war, all of Germany was starving. Ma and Lisa got only thin soup and hard black bread to eat. It was a difficult and lonely time for them.

"Meanwhile, I and the children were put on board another ship, the *Melitta*, which brought us safely to

Montreal. Finally, we were in this new country, Canada. We felt safe at last!

"During the long days on the train I wondered how I would support all of us. I had a good education and was fluent in German and Russian but not in English. I knew only that the train was taking us to a little town in Manitoba named Altona.

"As the train pulled into Altona, I noticed a crowd of people at the station. They were local farmers who came to pick up immigrants to work for them during the busy harvesting season.

"Everything seemed very strange as the children and I settled down on a bench to wait. We wondered who would choose us. I was relieved to hear some of the farmers speaking German. Time and again a farmer chose a family to go with them. Soon all the other families were taken and we were left alone in the waiting room. I realized that the farmers all picked families with a mother to take care of the children. Because we had no mother, we were not chosen. The afternoon dragged on. The children were hungry but we had no place to go. While I was wondering where to get food for the children, a stout elderly farmer in blue overalls entered to pick up a parcel. He seemed surprised to see us. Chewing on a blade of straw he looked us over. "What, you still here? Nobody picked you? No mother? Menschenskinder, this will never do!"

Still chewing the blade of straw, he eyed the pathetic huddle of children thoughtfully. There were Margaret, age fourteen, Mary, thirteen, Jacob, twelve, George (we always called him Gerd), ten, down to Arn, five years old.

"My name is Hildebrand from Sommerfeld. Let's see, perhaps you can work for me and keep the little fellow with you. We'll divide the other children among my married sons. They all have young families and could use help with the little ones. Now we'll go home to Sommerfeld. Come children, pile into my car! I think you could use a hearty supper!"

"The boys could hardly believe their ears! To ride in a car! Forgetting their shyness, the boys dashed ahead. Quick as a flash Arn secured the front seat. It was a shiny Ford car with leather curtains all around. Mr. Hildebrand edged himself and his right leg into the driver's seat and grabbing the left pant hoisted up the other leg. Away we went to Sommerfeld."

"To me that car was the most exciting thing in the world," Gerd added, "but I also remember that nothing ever tasted so good as that supper of beans and sausage. We had never seen such a big bowl of beans. We ate and ate and ate! Whenever I eat beans now I always remember the kind Hildebrands of Sommerfeld!"

"And that was our first day in Manitoba," Pa ended his story.

"What happened next Pa?" Lisa asked.

The Skunk

The next story was about Pa's first adventure in Manitoba. Lisa was glad that Pa could laugh about it now as he related the experience.

"That first year without Ma was a long, lonely time for the children, especially for Arn who was only five years old. His brothers and sisters were away working on the neighboring farms. I came home late at night, tired after a hard day in the fields, so Arn did not see me often.

"After harvesting, Mr. Hildebrand did not need me anymore. It was important to me to have the children together as a family again. Mr. Hildebrand was very helpful. He got permission from the school board for us to live in the vacant teacherage nearby. It had not been used for some time and needed a thorough cleaning.

"Accompanied by some neighboring farmers, Mr. Hildebrand took me to check out the little house. Mr. Hildebrand unlocked the door that led directly into the cellar. After one look he beat a hasty retreat.

"'Skunk,' he warned. 'There's a skunk in the basement!'

"His words had an electrifying effect on the men present. They backed away with one accord.

"I was puzzled and so asked, 'How big is it?'

"'About the size of a cat,' was the reply.

"Surely grown men could not be afraid of an animal

the size of a cat! No one made a move. Clearly it was my duty to deal with this problem. After all it was to be our home.

"I picked up a heavy stick and went to the door. The men stepped back, unbelief on their faces. I shook my head in puzzlement, opened the door and boldly proceeded down the steps.

"There was a moment of profound and utter silence. Then a terrible crash as I tore up the steps, white as a sheet. Wildly gasping for air, I flung myself on the grass. Then making a desperate dash for the nearby creek, I plunged into the water, dousing myself over and over to escape the suffocating odor.

"At last, panting and gasping, I collapsed on the grassy bank. A circle of perplexed faces looked down on me.

"'You did not know about skunks?' they asked in astonishment.

"'Never heard of them. They are not known in Europe,' I managed feebly.

"The little house had to be aired for a long time before we could move in!"

Ma Comes To Canada

Pa laughed about the skunk episode now, although he had felt quite ill for a few days. He was in a storytelling mood, and so continued with another story. As soon as he started, Lisa smiled. This was her favorite story.

"After the teacherage was cleaned up, I and the children moved in. The rooms were very drab and contained only the barest of furniture but it was so good to all be together again. Margaret and Mary did their very best to cook and clean and mend. The farmers occasionally brought potatoes, cabbages, carrots, sometimes eggs and smoked sausages, or beef bones for soup. Margaret could make good soup from almost anything. Mary and Margaret always remembered the soup from the shrivelled old beet that Ma had cooked when they were starving in Russia.

"The boys started school. I did the hard jobs, chopping wood and repairing broken windows and doors. Everyone was busy. I made sure that breakfast was a special time for family devotions, just as if Ma were there, and that grace was said before every meal. When the boys grumbled I would say, 'Saying grace is simply a courtesy and sign of good manners. Don't ever forget that!'

"Mary had taught herself to bake bread. I was very proud of her. Margaret's soup and Mary's bread made a good supper.

"Often, after supper we gathered around the dim light of the oil lamp, sitting very quietly. The room seemed strangely bare. The black night pushed against the window panes, wanting to enter. Loneliness seemed to creep out of the drafty walls and floorboards, slowly spreading throughout the room.

"Finally I would say, 'Well, children, let's sing,' and then begin their favorite round song:
    Oh wie wohl ist mir am Abend
    Mir am Abend
    Wenn zur Ruh die Glocken laüten
    Glocken laüten
    Bim bam bim bam!

    O how lovely is the evening
    Is the evening
    When the bells are sweetly ringing
    Sweetly ringing
    Ding, dong, ding, dong!

"Margaret and Mary chimed in, bravely carrying the melody. Arn piped up to carry his part. But what should have been a glorious chiming of bells, often petered out pitifully. One by one, the children quietly slipped into their beds, covering up their tears of longing. After all, they thought I had enough problems. They had stopped asking when Ma would come.

"Far into the night I would sit in the dim room thinking. When would Ma come? Her letters sounded hopeful. But with meager rations in Germany, her cure could not be speedy. If I could manage the winter, I would find work again in summer. But the huge immigration debt to the C.P.R. company, plus the already mounting interest always loomed so large. When could I ever manage to begin payment on that? And if I failed to meet the payment, would we all be sent back? I tried to push the idea out of my mind. I could not allow myself to think about that!

"Then in spring the good news came. Ma and the baby were coming! Mr. Hildebrand and I went to get them from the station to the Hildebrand home. Ma looked so thin and worn, her eyes and cheeks hollow. Gerd and Arn were scared. She had been away so long, she seemed like a stranger. And there were tears in her eyes, but the children did not know they were tears of joy and relief. They felt shy and strange with her. They turned their attention to the baby, a skinny little thing running around curiously, inspecting everything. The last time they had seen her she was just a baby, and now she could walk and talk! Seeing the chickens, she ran closer to watch them, but they scattered in all directions with agitated cries of tuk-tuk-tuk! Everyone laughed at her surprise.

"Arn took little Lisa to the barn to see the new lambs. Then Jacob carried her to the granary and set her into the huge bins filled with wheat. With great delight Lisa scooped handfuls of the smooth grain, dug big hollows, and buried her legs in the wheat. Gerd took her to the garden swing, and pushed her gently.

"It was easier for the children to hug a little girl than to hug their Ma, who still seemed a bit of a stranger.

"After a few days the children discovered that baby Lisa could not only walk and talk, but could sing a number of songs. During the long, lonely days in Germany, Ma had taught her dozens of German folk songs. Lisa sang gladly at the drop of a hat. Her favorite was:

1. Kommt ein Vogel geflogen
   Setzt sich nieder auf mein Fuss
   Hat ein Brieflein im Schnabel
   Von Mama einen Gruss!

2. Liebes Vöglein flieg weiter
   Nimm ein Gruss mit und ein Kuss
   Denn ich kann dich nicht begleiten
   Weil ich hierbleiben muss!

Came a little bird flying
Settled down on my shoe
In its beak held a letter
From my mamma, greetings true!

Little birdie, take my message
It will tell her of my love
Since I cannot be with her
Wish her blessings from above.

"News about the singing child, not even two years old, quickly made the rounds. Wherever we went Lisa was asked to sing her songs. She quickly learned that songs meant treats from some kind gentleman's pocket, so she sang gladly and freely!

"Do you remember that Lisa?" Pa asked as he turned to her. "Especially how Mr. Hildebrand was so generous and always had a treat for you?"

"Oh yes, Pa," Lisa replied excitedly. "I certainly loved those treats!"

A chalice for Christmas

Lisa was very sorry when Gerd and Arn laid aside their violin-making project when school began in September. The difficulties in building a violin became increasingly apparent. The boys had been pleased with the top and back and even the f-holes were quite successful. The curves of the side pieces created a big problem and would take a great deal of time. This was discouraging. Now that school was in session, their spare hours were filled with chores and homework. Besides, something very special had come into the house to claim their attention.

Lisa and Leni were always happy to see Jacob come home from Reinland where he worked for a farmer. He was always full of surprises, bringing a few pieces of licorice, a pretty post card or a used magazine with pictures in it.

This day Jacob came home with a big, square wooden box. It was an old gramophone that he had traded for some rabbit skins. As he set it on the kitchen table everyone crowded around to see. Jacob lifted the heavy wooden lid and slipped a shiny black tube over a metal arm. He wound the crank on the side of the box and carefully lowered the metal arm with the needle underneath.

The disc began turning and the sounds of 'Lead Kindly Light' filled the room. The label said 'Knickerbocker Male Quartet.'

"This one says 'Ave Maria.' The singer's name is Caruso and there is another name, Mischa Elman," Arn said slowly, trying to read the faint labels. A sound such as they never heard before filled the room as Caruso's voice and Elman's violin joined in the beautiful 'Ava Maria.'

They sat in awe and wonder as Jacob selected another disc named 'Minuet and Valse' by Bluette, played by Kathleen Parlow. Again the strains of a violin, so sweet and enticing, left them in reverent silence. Arn had not dreamed such sounds were humanly possible here on earth. Could such brilliance come from a violin? Was this dream or reality? Was it possible to learn to play like that? He and Gerd often went over to Kuhl's to hear the radio programs of Roy Rogers and some country fiddlers. But never had he heard anything like this!

There were many more discs with wonderful singers with strange names like Galli Curci, Alma Gluck, Tito Schipa. But Arn always went back to the violin discs. Arn had never heard of Kathleen Parlow but he had read about Fritz Kreisler. He must sound even more wonderful.

"Just imagine hearing Fritz Kreisler," Arn burst out. "He is a great Austrian violinist. I read that when he appears on stage, people already weep before he even plays! We must try to get a disc of Kreisler. If he should ever come to Winnipeg I would walk all the way to hear him!"

Lisa thought almost a hundred miles would be a very long walk.

"You know, Kathleen Parlow is a wonderful violinist, but from what I read if Fritz Kreisler had played this it would be even better!" Arn pronounced in his enthusiasm.

They all laughed, thinking of Uncle Isaac, who claimed that Brahms *'Wiegenlied'* would have been even better if Schubert had written it!

Still, Arn did not even have a violin of his own. Lisa had almost forgotten about the secret of the Eaton's catalogue violin. she had asked Pa about it a while ago but he had only shaken his head. Now all she could do was wish very hard that the secret would come true.

Soon Lisa had time to think about Christmas only. School days were filled with songs, recitations and plays to practise for the Christmas concert. Every day brought tiny tingles of delight at the very thought of Christmas. When she came home from school one day, she saw a heaping mound of peppernuts brown with molasses and spices, fresh out of the oven. Ma usually stored them in the big stone crock in the pantry, but these had just been baked. Lisa loved peppernuts and scooped up a handful for a snack. Ma also baked rich golden honey cookies, spicy, dark lebkuchen in a white glaze, and sugar cookies with red sugar on top. Lisa's favorites were the light feathery peppermint cookies that left a cool minty flavor on her tongue.

And one day Ma made her special Christmas candy. In a large pot she mixed 1 cup of milk, 2/3 cup cocoa and 4 cups sugar. This was to simmer for a few minutes. As Ma stirred with a long wooden spoon, she added 1 cup butter, some vanilla and 2 cups of flour. Now it was hard to stir, so Gerd helped to mix it till it was smooth. Ma poured it into a large pan to cool. Once it was cool, they could each have one square of the rich chocolate fudge before Ma put it away. The fragrance of honey, cinnamon, peppermint and chocolate filled the whole house, lingering pleasantly in every room.

In her spare time Lisa was busy drawing pictures for Christmas gifts for Ma and Pa. Her favorite was the Bethlehem scene with Joseph and Mary and the child. It took a long time to do the faces; they were so hard to get right. If only she could make the faces as beautiful as those in 'Madonna of the Chair' in Arn's old reader. But she made up for the faces by giving the garments the brightest shades of blue and red. The crayons always left a gritty residue. If she had water paints the colors would be so much brighter and clearer! She knew that Pa would like her present very much so she kept on trying.

Leni was making a picture too. She did not like to draw faces so she made a Christmas tree with lots of decorations on it. She used all the colors of the crayon box. She thought Ma would like hers best.

Finally Christmas Eve arrived. They all walked down the snowy road through the starry night, on their way to the Christmas program.

The schoolroom was filling with parents and friends, who greeted one another as they settled down. Lisa's class sat in the second row. She felt very festive as she smoothed down her red and black checked dress trimmed with red braid. Tante Anna had sewed the same dresses for both Leni and Lisa, with material from Janzen's store in Winkler.

Lisa forgot about her dress as she looked into the corner at the Christmas tree reaching right up to the ceiling. The flickering flames of countless white wax candles lit up the shiny tinsel and glass ornaments. She found herself in the choir of children singing, 'Sweetly the Bells are Ringing.'

There were readings and recitations. Then the curtains opened on the stage and, oh truly, 'the Glory of the Lord shone all about them!' For there appeared three angels in snowy robes with shimmering feathery wings of purest white, whose tips reached the floor. As the kneeling shepherds gazed at the sight, a sound of admiration and astonishment rose from the audience. Lisa sat entranced, feeling an ache at the beauty of it. Then the angels sang *'Ehre sei Gott in der Hohe!'* (Glory to God in the Highest), and disappeared as they made way for the manger scene.

On the way home Lisa could not join in the excited chatter of her friends. She kept thinking about the angels and the songs and the tree.

In the kitchen Leni was already setting out the biggest plate she could find. Arn selected Ma's big enamelled baking bowl, hoping it would be filled with goodies right to the top by Santa. They all teased him about it.

Later in bed Lisa could only think about the angels. Had it been real? Suddenly she was surrounded by angels hovering over her bed and singing. As she reached out she found herself carried through the starry night, higher and higher.

Suddenly the angels disappeared and she was falling through space. With a bump she found herself back in bed. It had been a dream after all and now it was Christmas morning! Already she heard stirrings. She jumped out of bed and ran to join the others. Entering the kitchen Lisa stopped and caught her breath.

In the centre of the kitchen table stood a little fir tree lit with gently flaming wax candles, multiplied many times by the reflections of the shiny glass ornaments. Her plate was filled with nuts and candy. Beside her plate was a shiny black metal box. She opened it to find, oh wonder, eight large squares of paints in rich gorgeous colors! As if in a dream, she picked up the paint brush. It was like holding a promise in her hand. All the things she could paint flashed through her mind. Maybe now she could even paint sunsets!

Leni was already munching goodies from her plate and exclaiming over her picture book of fairy tales.

Sleepily, Arn came in to inspect his big baking bowl. It was not filled to the top but contained the same amount as the other plates. Well, Santa was certainly fair, he thought. He looked beside the bowl expecting the usual gift of socks and mittens.

But what was this? There was a long black case with shiny metal clasps. Arn looked at it in shocked surprise. Surely it could not be? But yes, it was! Full of wonder he slowly undid the metal clasps.

Arn caught his breath. There it was, a golden brown violin, shiny in its newness, complete with strings, pegs and bridge. The entire case was lined in rich blue

felt. It held a violin bow and a box of rosin. And underneath lay an illustrated instruction book.

Gerd saw the book first, and picked it up. He read the title, "The E-Z Violin Method."

What riches! Trembling with excitement, Arn timidly plucked the strings. To him it was a holy chalice filled with all his dreams. Still speechless, he handed it to Pa, feeling that the moment called for some ceremony.

Turning the pages carefully, Pa tuned the very new strings. He put rosin on the bow and gently fingered 'O Come Little Children.' It was the very first tune on the Eaton's catalogue violin.

They all gathered to listen and admire. Jacob and Gerd were content with their new socks and mitts. After all, the violin was a gift for the whole family to enjoy.

So the secret had come true after all, Lisa thought, and all her wishing had helped. How carefully Ma must have saved her egg and butter money! Now she remembered that for a long time the family had spread bacon crackles instead of butter on their bread.

Lisa ran to Ma stirring the porridge for breakfast at the kitchen stove. Ma only smiled her usual cheerful smile, but Lisa knew Ma had given up her frilly curtains.

Preparing for New Year's

"This is the last day of the year in Gnadenthal and all over the world," Pa announced coming in from the barn. Lisa had not thought about that.

"Even in China?" she asked.

"Even in China and India and Australia. Not every country celebrates Christmas but New Year is observed everywhere."

"It seems to make the whole world more real. Countries can wish each other 'Happy New Year' around the world," said Lisa, pleased at the thought. It was a friendly feeling.

Stirring the crock of yeast sponge mixed the night before, Ma laughed at Lisa's remark. She added flour, milk, sugar, eggs and butter and plenty of raisins, then set the batter aside to rise until double in bulk.

The best part would come later in the afternoon. Ma heated cooking fat in the big iron kettle. Then she dropped spoonfuls of raisin batter into the bubbling fat. Lisa and Leni watched in fascination as the white lumps slowly turned a golden brown forming curious shapes of all varieties, then flipped themselves over to cook evenly. They were done quickly and Ma fished out the first ones for the girls to sample. They were brown and crusty, studded with raisins and deliciously soft and sweet on the inside.

The pile of golden fritters grew and grew. As Ma ladled them out on a large baking pan, they filled the

whole house with a sweet fruity fragrance. In fact, from every house in Gnadenthal the same tempting aroma issued until, by late afternoon, the whole village seemed wrapped in an invisible cloud of fritter vapor, proclaiming comfort and goodwill.

In Gnadenthal and all the other villages it was considered inconceivable to usher in the New Year without these traditional *Neujahrskuchen* (New Year's Fritters).

Soon they heard the boys with a great commotion of talk and laughter in the barn hallway noisily stamping snow off their heavy boots.

"The smell tempted us—came all the way clear to the granary," Jacob laughed, as they settled down at the kitchen table.

"Pity it's only once a year we get this treat," Gerd lamented, biting into the crispy brown fritter.

Ma put out the china sugar bowl. "We used to dip the hot fritters in sugar," she laughed.

"Such extravagance, no sugar needed for these!" Pa admonished as he reached for the enamelled coffee pot warming on the back of the stove.

"Pa you said it was New Year's Eve all over the world. Do you think that in every house in the world they are making *Neujahrskuchen* today?"

"Not in China, nor in Africa," Arn laughed.

"Or in Russia," Pa said quietly. Lisa saw a look of pain cross his face briefly. She understood vaguely, knowing only that people were dying of hunger in that country. All were quiet for a moment.

"I'll be glad when these are done," Ma sighed, spooning the last of the batter into the sizzling fat. She looked flushed and tired.

"This takes all day, and there is still so much to do! Then we have to get ready for *Sylvester Abend* (New Year's Eve) tonight.

"Well," Pa announced, "I'm not shaving again this year!"

Leni looked concerned. Would Pa grow a beard?

"Yes, and I refuse to take another bath this year!"

Jacob proclaimed firmly. Leni brightened at this.

"No bath all year?" Leni burst out hopefully at the thought of such a possibility. She especially disliked having her hair washed and soap in her eyes.

They all laughed.

"Of course!" Lisa thought. "Tomorrow is next year!"

Bringing in the New Year

As they walked to church that night, Lisa hoped for a good seat. She wanted to see everything!

Most of the seats were taken, men on one side of the aisle, women on the other. Lisa slipped in beside Lili in the front row. She and Lili had permission to stay for the entire program. It would be wonderful to enjoy it together! They both turned at the commotion behind them. A row of boys had noisily settled in the very back. Now they were unceremoniously relegated to the front bench to be under the direct observation of their elders. To alleviate this injustice they resorted to sly kicks and scuffles, making faces at each other behind the hymnals. Jack, his curly brown hair cropped short, his cousin Dave, his friends David, Henry and Walter, all squirmed uncomfortably in their unnatural attire of Sunday best.

In spite of the transformation that thorough scrubbing had wrought, rendering their faces innocent and cherubic, Lisa dared only guess at the contents of their pockets. It was likely an assortment of string, sunflower seeds, rubber rings, matches and carefully collected cigarette butts, the latter precious and hard to come by.

Turning to Lili for comment, Lisa heard the first song announced to begin the service. After clearing his throat, the minister welcomed the congregation, encouraging one and all to look back and meditate on the past year. How had it been meaningful? Had we indeed counted all our blessings? Would anyone like to share?

A great silence descended. Lisa knew that the year had been difficult for all. Crops had failed and many, including Pa, could not make their payments. According to Pa that meant the interest mounted, increasing the debt. And it was not only the debt on the farm but also the large immigration debt to the C.P.R.

Slowly Mr. Enns arose, "I thank God for bringing us to this country to live in peace, without fear!"

"We thank God for good health in the past year," said Mrs. Epp, a tiny widow struggling to support her four children. Their house was bare and drafty and their food was mainly garden vegetables and bread. Her two sons, one not yet a teenager, did heavy farm chores for neighbors in order to buy shoes and the barest necessities. Yet Mrs. Epp was thankful. How could she be thankful, Lisa wondered. There was so much to think about as the service continued.

Mrs. Hamm arose, struggling with tears. Their baby had died of scarlet fever, but she was grateful the other children had been spared. Lisa felt a lump in her throat as she remembered the tiny white form in the small coffin.

The moment all were waiting for arrived. Every New Year's Eve, Mr. Lepp rose for a confession of sins, adding new ones each year. With anguished outpouring, he asked for divine forgiveness, alluding to deep and dark transgressions in the past. No, he would not name his sins, since the Almighty knew what a sinner he was. Overcome with emotion he paused, unable to continue for the moment. With a flourish of his handkerchief he wiped his eyes. Blowing his nose vigorously, he began to earnestly exhort and urge one and all to repent and confess. He ended with a plea to the congregation in general for forgiveness if there should be any reason for such!

Lisa wondered what his transgressions were.

Strangely enough, nobody seemed to know or be overly concerned. But the annual episode added a real touch of drama to the service.

After a short break, the *Jugendverein* (Youth Group) program began. The theme was still spiritual with the choir choosing songs more dramatic in nature like 'The Ninety and Nine.' 'The Ten Virgins,' a parable in drama form, was the main feature. Lisa found herself completely absorbed in the soul stirring story, in which the virgins look forward to meeting the groom. Only five had taken the trouble to fill their lamps with oil. Too late the other virgins hurried to get oil, but alas when they arrived the door was shut!

The effect on the congregation was profound. Many were deeply moved. How fitting a theme for the last day of the year! Many a silent vow was made.

After the closing prayer, Lisa and Leni breathed a sigh of relief. Now they could enjoy the fun part of the evening, the Literary, a monthly presentation. For this program, the conductor chose traditional well-loved songs, 'Still ruht der See,' 'Die Kapelle' and Lisa's favorite, 'Lindenbaum.' Tonight the choir sang a new song, 'Das Leben ist ja nur ein Traum' (Life is but a Dream) with Tina singing the solo part in her high sweet voice. It was so beautiful!

Now came the highlight, the reading of the Journal, the monthly work of four young collaborators, which was awaited with great anticipation. This document, intended to be of a high and lofty literary nature, contained gems of great authors and eventful world news. However, it was not beneath recording village events such as the visit of the Peters family from Blumenort; the incident of the runaway team causing a near accident; a gathering of the Penner family for Grandpa's birthday; the arrival of twin calves to the Pauls' best milk cow; the Kuhls' trip to Winnipeg in their new car.

The lofty tone of the Journal at times became less so when mischievous authors alluded to certain couples seen walking down the willow path called

'Lovers' Lane' on a starry night. Lisa and Lili, totally intrigued with these allusions, surreptitiously tried to guess. This was highly romantic and needed much discussion and investigation.

Sometimes the Journal included riddles, leaving the audience guessing, and sometimes even jokes, in good taste of course, causing quiet chuckles. All in all, the Journal proved to be a well-balanced presentation of interest to young and old.

Now Jacob rendered a stirring recitation of *"Erlking"* by Goethe, outdoing himself in his love for drama and leaving his audience enthralled.

Winding up the program, the orchestra took its turn. The girls sat in front with their guitars, each adorned with a great red bow, in perfect alignment. Behind them stood the violinists and to the left the mandolin players. And behind them all was Mr. Kuhl with his big bass fiddle. It had no bow, but he played the bass line just plucking the strings, producing a drum effect. The guitars strummed softly, the violins sang, the mandolins tremoled and the bass fiddle thumped in a glorious blending of harmony. Sometimes the congregation joined in singing 'The Beautiful Stream,' or 'Somewhere,' but Lisa liked it best with only the instruments. She still was too young, but maybe someday she too would play a guitar. She felt a shiver of joy at the thought!

The families with little ones now prepared to go home. For the first time, Lisa and Lili had permission to stay for the entire evening.

Helen, considered the best coffee maker in her group, had prepared huge amounts of coffee at home. The young men transported it to church in large milk cans. Baskets containing cups were passed along. The choir girls made the rounds pouring coffee from tin kettles. Large platters of *Neujahrskuchen,* honey cake and peppermint cookies were passed around. Lisa and Lili had coffee and cookies, too. It was a little overwhelming to be part of this adult late-night event. With great interest they observed the young people joking and teasing. Some young couples were already going together seriously. The girls wondered what it would be like 'going' with some boy. Lisa couldn't imagine. After all, she and Lili had decided to wait until a prince came along, someone far away from Europe where royalty lived.

Finally cups were collected in baskets and the crumbs swept up. Lisa was growing sleepy. It was hard to stay awake, but she did not want to miss the New Year.

Young Frank, the youth leader, stepped forward. He was a very gifted speaker. As he spoke the atmosphere became charged. A New Year was on the threshold. Was each and every one prepared to face it with a clear conscience? Had each settled his affairs? What if this were the last hour? Yet, there was still time for change and renewal. Earnestly he implored each and everyone to search his or her heart.

Lisa too must search her heart. How should she change her ways? She wished she knew exactly. With a stab of guilt she realized how often she kept on reading when Ma called her to help out; and how often she resented sharing with Leni, or how often she secretly enjoyed a storybook under her school desk during arithmetic.

Lisa glanced toward the men's side. Of what sins did they need to repent? And what could they possibly change about their ways? What evil could there be in the same chores every one did each day? She could not imagine any one stealing or fighting, or, horrors, being drunk! She had never heard of a drunk person in the village, but secretly wondered what it was like.

They were admonished to remember this might be their last hour on earth. In the end each and every one would be made accountable. The minutes ticked away, fraught with emotion and soul-searching.

Lisa was profoundly moved as though she were part of a big drama. She was still trying to remember her worst sins. Before she came to a proper conclusion, the speaker pronounced the Amen.

Frank now asked the assembly to join in singing the stirring song:

    Siehe, die Uhr ist schon weit nach elf
    Nur fünf Minuten, dann schlägt sie zwölf!
    See the time is now past eleven
    In five more minutes it will strike twelve!

There was total and utter silence. Then quietly a voice announced, "The New Year has come!"

New Year's Day

Lisa felt she could never open her eyes and wake up again, her eyelids were so heavy. Again she heard knocking and commotion on the kitchen door. Trying to shake her drowsiness, Lisa heard voices and singing and then laughter. Finally, Lisa made her way to the kitchen. The cool air rushing in through the open door awakened her fully. A group of youngsters in woolly toques and scarves were chanting:

Eck sach den Schornsteen ruacke
Eck wisst uck wout jie muacke
Scheene Niejooschkuacke
Jeav jie mie eene, sto eck stell,
Jeav jie mie twee, fang eck aun to goane
Jeav jie mie dree on vea tojlick
Dann wensch eck junt
Daut gaunze Himmelrick!

I saw your chimney smoking
I knew what you were cooking
New Year's fritters making.
Give me one and I stand still
Give me two and I start to go
Give me three and four together
I wish you heaven's blessings and good weather!

Laughing, Ma invited them in and shut the door. Lisa, tousled and groggy, smiled at the happy faces.

They held brown paper bags in their mittened hands. Mother dropped *Neujahrskuchen* and candy into each bag. Thanking Ma politely they were off to make the rounds for more goodies.

At breakfast Ma laughed, telling Pa and the boys about the morning visitors. "Making the rounds on New Year's Day is an old European custom. In the Russian villages not only the children but the adults too went from door to door with good wishes. They were rewarded with small gifts or pennies and in turn threw a handful of grain on the floor for good luck as they left. It was a friendly custom!"

After the late night events, breakfast was a leisurely and relaxed time. Dreamily, Lisa listened to the boys' lively discussion of the drama and the Journal. Jacob had come in even later. They all pretended not to know that he had walked Tina home.

Lisa was still awed by her first New Year's Eve experience. She would never forget it as long as she lived. This afternoon she and Lili would have a wonderful time discussing every minute of it in detail. But now it was time for her to recite her New Year's Wish for Ma and Pa. Leni could still recite the short one. Being older, Lisa was expected to learn a longer one. She remembered feeling all choked up and fighting tears on these occasions. If she cried, her brothers would be amused. Not anymore! She would just think about doing a good job for Ma and Pa. So she began.

> Mit Gott ins neue Jahr
> Ins neue Jahr mit frohem Mut!
> Glaub' fest: Was kommen mag, ist gut,
> Denn Einer sitzt im Regiment
> Der all deine Nöte kennt,
> Der höher denkt und weiter schaut,
> Dein Glück mit heil'gen Händen baut,
> Dir taglich neue Kräfte schenkt
> Und jedes Leid zum Besten lenkt,
> Der ewig ist und ewig war,
> Geht mit dir auch im neuen Jahr.

> With God in the New Year
> Welcome the New Year with happy mood
> Firmly believe that it will be good
> Who knows your needs and is at hand
> To guide, protect and plan for you
> That hopes for the future may come true;
> Who daily promises strength anew
> In every heartache comforts you
> May he, who eternal was and is
> Direct and guide you in His ways.

She could tell Ma and Pa were pleased and she felt that her brothers were proud of her although they would never admit it. That's what brothers were like!

Sometimes she wished she could give Ma and Pa a beautiful gift, such as a velvet cushion or a crystal vase like she had seen at Lili's house. But Pa said the New Year's Wish was the best gift they could get because nobody could ever take it away from them. Just like the songs and stories that would be her very own for always, Lisa thought.

Next year she would learn a longer wish for Ma and Pa.

Valentine's Day Preparations

Lisa and Leni were lost in a flurry of activity preparing for Valentine's Day. Night after night was spent creating colorful valentines for all their friends at school.

The kitchen table was covered with paper, glue and crayons, so that Ma had to move her mending closer to Pa. Although he felt a little crowded, nothing could distract him from his reading, especially when it was Dostoyevsky. Lisa could not see why anyone would care to read Russian, but Pa patiently explained that it was a beautiful poetic language.

Carefully Lisa folded a sheet of white paper to cut out a double heart. She wished for red paper, but this had to do. In the centre of the heart she cut two lines across and one down, folding back the flaps to make little shutters. She cut out a pretty face from the Eaton's catalogue and glued it on the second heart, so the face looked out when the shutters were opened. On each shutter she colored a little red heart and printed I LOVE YOU around the frame.

Leni was all pink in her face, furiously coloring her cut-out hearts. Since she had no red paper she used lots of crayon for color. The wax always left a gritty residue, so Lisa made small hearts instead, surrounded by fancy green vines.

"I'll make a valentine for everyone in my class, except boys of course," Lisa explained to Ma. You

simply did not send valentines to boys!

"Well, I'll have to work very hard if I want to make one for every girl in my class. I wish I would get at least one bought one. Lisa got a bought one from Abe last year. Abe really likes you. I suppose you'll get one again this year," Leni said as she worked on a heart for her teacher. She chose the prettiest face in the catalogue to put in the valentine window. How pleased her teacher would be!

Secretly, Lisa too hoped for a bought valentine. It would be special.

Looking up for a moment, Pa saw Leni's face all flushed from cutting and coloring. He turned to Lisa and asked, "How about getting something from the apple barrel, owl?"

Seeing Lisa hesitate, Pa quickly added, "I'll go myself, owl, I know my way in the dark!"

Lisa was relieved. She was afraid to go into the dark earthen cellar. There was a big barrel of dills in brine, another of pickled watermelon beside the apple barrel. There were bins of cabbages, turnips and beets. You never knew what lurked behind those bins and barrels. Arn had strongly hinted at all kinds of crawly creatures that might be lying in wait.

"Here, children, have a rosy 'sheepshead'," Pa announced as he set a bowl of apples on the table. The barrel that Pa brought from Plum Coulee every winter contained all sizes and shapes of apples from MacIntosh to Russets. Now he had picked those the girls liked best, 'sheepsheads.'

Leni bit into the rosy translucent skin of an apple almost as big as her face. It was wonderful to sink the teeth into the sweet crunchy texture, releasing a delicious fragrance which Lisa could only describe as 'appley.'

Watching Leni crunching through her apple, Pa laughed, "What would our little huppup do without apples?"

She didn't know what 'huppup' meant but it didn't matter.

"Ma, what did you do for Valentine's Day when you went to school?" Lisa asked.

"We didn't have Valentine's then. But we had autograph albums in which we exchanged verses. I still have one that I brought from Germany."

Ma went to get the album from the wooden chest. It had an old red leather cover with an engraved picture with golden trellises.

Carefully the girls turned the pages. They were such beautiful pages, in delicate shades of pink, blue and green. The verses, in spidery Gothic script with artistic flourishes, had the elegance of another era. For Ma the album brought back memories of a difficult time.

"When we left Russia to go to Canada, all the immigrants were held in South Hampton for health inspections. Pa and the children could go on to Canada, but I was sent back to Germany for eye treatments. Because Lisa was still a baby, I took her with me. The old army barracks at Lager Lechfeld were very crowded. Lisa and I lived in a little space partitioned off by blankets. I had painful eye treatments every day. Because of the meagre rations of thin soup and black bread, my health did not improve quickly. I made friends with other families who were all anxiously waiting to go to Canada.

"Since I had trouble with my teeth, I could not eat the hard crusts, so I saved them. When I had a small pail full of crusts I went down to the village. Germany was very poor at that time and many people were starving, so I gave the crusts away. One time a village woman gave me this old album. She insisted that I keep it as a thank you for the crusts.

"As the album made the rounds in the barracks, each friend wrote a special verse for me. We had shared a difficult time together and might not see each other again. Today these verses bring back treasured memories about each person."

The Kroeger clock ticked away as the family listened to Ma. Sometimes Leni wished the clock would stop,

Zur Ehrendes Gott dein Tagwerk,
Sein Hoffnung deim Morgen,
Sein Lieben deinem Kampf,
Seine Anker das Grab.

Zum für Erinnerung
an
Gerhard Egg

Laupar Inftitut,
30. Mai 1924

especially at bedtime. She still had so many valentines to make.

"Clean up your papers, huppup, it's your bedtime and tomorrow is another day," Pa reminded, closing his Dostoyevsky.

As Lisa gathered up her papers she kept wishing for an autograph album of her very own.

Easter

It would be the most exciting Easter of her eleven years, Lisa thought, stepping out on the front porch. The sun was already warming the world.

She heard the trill of a meadowlark in the field. So brilliant, it seemed to hang in the air. If she could see the sound, it would be like silver spirals against the blue sky! Again and again she thrilled to the silvery song. She wondered what happened to the beautiful sound. Where did it go? With a rush of joy she wanted to hold out her hand and capture the song and make it her very own. She could not catch the song, but the joy would stay!

Again Lisa looked at the sky, reassured that the weather would be perfect for this special day! If only the grownups would hurry!

Rover was lying in a warm patch of sun near the barn. Wagging his tail he trotted up to Lisa.

"He smiles with his tail," thought Lisa fondly, and laughed out loud. Hugging Rover, she pulled him down beside her on the porch. Furiously thumping the porch with his tail, he kept licking her face over and over.

"Today we hunt for Easter eggs and then we have egg rolling at church," she laughed, scratching his back.

"But first you must have your breakfast. Let's see if the milking is done."

Entering the barn she heard the swish of milk flowing into a pail. His head against the brown flank of Bessie, her brother Jacob was filling the pail between his knees with frothy white milk. Once in a while he mischievously aimed a stream of milk at the waiting cats, Mietz and Max. To them this was no joking matter. Motionless, eyes inscrutable, they ignored him, knowing full well they would get a bowlful later.

At the sight of Rover, their eyes narrowed into mere slits as they pretended to disappear without disappearing. Rover had long ago given up trying to figure out these frustrating creatures. As long as he was Lisa's favorite, all was well.

Lisa left him to enter the little hallway that led directly to the kitchen. She always enjoyed stepping into the kitchen with its blue and white checkered design painted on the wooden floor.

The long wooden table was already set for breakfast with a heaping plate of golden *zwieback* at each end. In the center sat a round shallow dish covered with thick green grass. Two weeks ago Ma had planted wheat in the dish, and it came up just in time for Easter, like a little green lawn. Placed among the thick blades of grass were eggs decorated with all colors of the rainbow. It was a lovely centerpiece.

Yesterday Ma hardboiled a dozen eggs. She poured some boiling water and a tablespoon of vinegar into three cups. Then she added some coloring — red, blue and yellow. While the eggs were still hot, Lisa and Leni put one in each cup, stirring gently with a teaspoon. Soon the egg turned a deep red or blue or yellow. Each following egg became paler and paler until there were many shades. At last Lisa mixed the blue and yellow to make green. Ma rubbed each egg with a bacon rind to make it shiny. Lisa and Leni could choose the prettiest eggs for their own.

The special holiday treat was the *Easter Paska* made with a very rich batter of eggs, butter and cream. Ma put mounds of yeast batter into containers of all shapes and sizes. Some were round bowls, tin

cups or cans, or little honey pails. After the *paska* was baked, ma spread white icing on top. Lisa and Leni sprinkled red sugar over the icing. The *paska* looked like tall oversized mushrooms with white icing dripping down the sides. The girls could choose one for their very own. Lisa put hers on a white china plate with the colored eggs around it and set it on the wide windowsill of the kitchen where everyone could see it.

Jacob came in with a foaming pail of milk ready for the separator. As he turned the handle round and round, the machine hummed busily, sending a stream of white milk from one spout and yellow cream from the other. Lisa always wondered how the machine could distinguish the two. Cousin Melitta and Leni came into the pantry to watch. Melitta, with her parents, Tante Anna and Uncle Isaac, had arrived from Winkler to spend Easter in Gnadenthal.

At last they all sat down to breakfast, Melitta between Lisa and Leni. Pa opened the Bible and read the Easter text. Ordinarily the reading seemed to be only a bunch of words. Today it was a real story about people proclaiming the happy news that Jesus had risen.

As Pa closed the Bible, he said, "In the Ukraine, Easter was a very special day. Many years ago I attended an Easter morning service in an old Ukrainian cathedral. Great crowds of people had come to worship. They were all standing through the services because there were no pews in Ukrainian churches. Worshippers felt it was disrespectful to sit down in the presence of God.

"At the end of the service the priest proclaimed three times, *'Chrystos Voskres!'* (Christ is risen!) And three times the crowd jubilantly replied, *'Voistynu Voskres!'* (He is indeed risen!)

"The joyous chanting and the ringing of the great bells made the experience unforgettable. Then the people kissed and hugged one another, repeating the beautiful greeting over and over with great joy. These warm loving people made me feel that truly God was in their midst. Of course soon after the revolution all churches in Russia were closed."

Tante Anna sighed, "That is a beautiful story. It makes me feel like singing together! We all know this one!"

>Dankt dem Herrn
>Mit frohem Mut
>Er is freundlich
>Er is gut
>Seine Güt ermüdet nie
>Ewig, ewig wehret sie!

It was a good song, but it was so hard to wait. Grownups took so much time when such exciting things were in store.

The girls spoke the table grace in unison rather quickly:

>Komm Herr Jesu
>Sei unser Gast
>Und segne
>Was Du uns
>Bescheret hast
>Amen

>Come Lord Jesus
>Be our guest
>And bless the food
>That Thou for us
>Prepared hast.
>Amen

Melitta pulled a *zwieback* apart. She spread the fluffy inside with thick, purple chokecherry jam and took a big bite. Ma poured freshly brewed coffee for the adults and passed around the feathery lemon flavored slices of *Easter paska*. Pa spread a slice of *paska* with sweet creamy cottage cheese from the big blue bowl and put it on Lisa's plate. She was too excited to eat it all so she shared it with Melitta.

While the grownups were still laughing and talking, the children urged, "Now can we hunt for Easter eggs?"

Tante Anna took charge, "We will hunt outdoors. Come into the front garden children!"

The ground was nice and dry and already covered with a fuzzy carpet of grass. They searched around the lilac bushes and the big maple trees near the fence. Behind the prickly gooseberry bush, Lisa found a tiny basket filled with two fluffy yellow chicks in a nest of colorful jelly beans. Leni found a little cage with two fuzzy baby birds. Melitta came up with a wee white furry bunny in a straw nest of colored candy. All the little animals looked almost real.

Never before had Lisa found such lovely surprises! Tante Anna had specially bought these for them at Janzen's Store in Winkler. Lisa and Leni thanked Tante Anna again and again, but Melitta thanked her only once. She was used to special treats!

Egg Rolling

Later they all walked down the road to the village church. Melitta wore a new, pale green, organdy dress with ruffles which her mother had sewed. Tante Anna looked lovely in a new dress of filmy flowered voile. Ma did not have a new dress but she looked elegant in her black moire dress and the black satin bow with her rich brown hair piled high.

Lisa knew most of the songs in the hymn book because Ma often sang them at home. Sometimes Lisa stopped during a hymn to listen to the harmony of all the voices. She especially liked the rumbling sound on the men's side, like many bass fiddles playing together. The strong sound made her feel safe and secure.

The choir sang joyful songs and the minister talked about all things becoming new at Easter. Lisa looked around at the people. Most of them did not have new clothes but their faces looked happy and somehow new.

After the closing prayer it was announced that the Egg Rolling would begin right after lunch. The teachers placed an assortment of gifts along the floor of the front wall of the church. Each child was given a colored egg to roll down the center of the aisle. Whatever the egg touched would be the child's prize. Parents and children watched eagerly. Lisa's egg rolled down the aisle hitting a big wooden Easter Egg decorated with brightly painted flowers. She thanked the teacher who handed it to her. He told her to pull it apart in the middle. Inside was another painted egg. She opened this one and there was another inside, and another, each one smaller than the one before. The last one was a wee egg with a tiny flower painted on it. Lisa's cheeks were all red from the many surprises! Melitta's prize was a small basket of colored candy eggs. Leni had a little nest of chocolate chicks. Lisa could not eat the wooden egg but she liked it the very best of all. She never got tired of opening and closing the different sized eggs. She let Melitta and Leni take turns too. All the children were happy because each had won a prize!

For Easter dinner there were platters of sliced, baked ham and bowls of big juicy meatballs fried the day before. In the center of the table sat a big china tureen filled with *plumemooss* (a cold fruit soup), with raisins, prunes, apples and apricots. It was delicious. For dessert, there was of course the decorated *Easter paska* and a big blue bowl with sweet, creamed cottage cheese.

Everybody helped to clear the table and wash the dishes. The grownups gathered in the *Grosse Stube* (Parlor) to sit on the straight wooden benches and chairs. Tante Anna recited some beautiful poems. She and Uncle Isaac started singing 'Lorelei' and all joined in, followed by 'Lindenbaum', 'Heidenröslein' and finally Brahmas' 'Wiegenlied.' Uncle Isaac loved Schubert's songs above any others.

"You know," he remarked, "it is said that Brahm's 'Wiegenlied' is the most famous lullaby in the world. But if Schubert had written it, it would be even more beautiful!"

Everybody laughed at Uncle Isaac's statement. Lisa thought and thought about it trying to figure it out. Then she laughed too!

Evening approached. From the west, sunrays like long soft fingers crept into the *Grosse Stube* filling it with a last gentle glow. Slowly the shadows lengthened as the strains of *Nach der Heimat möcht ich wieder* died away.

> Nach der Heimat möcht ich wieder
> Nach dem teuren Vaterort
> Wo man singt so schöne Lieder
> Wo man hört manch süsses Wort
>
> Teure Heimat, sei gegrüsst
> In der Ferne sei gegrüsst
> Sei gegrüsst in weiter Ferne
> Teure Heimat, sei gegrüsst!
>
> To my homeland I would wander
> To my cherished fatherland
> Where you hear such joyous singing,
> Friends are walking hand in hand.
>
> Lovely homeland, hear my longing
> Far away from distant shore
> I shall hold you oh my homeland
> In my heart for evermore.

In that moment of silence a sweet, sad sound drifted through the open windows. It was the mourning dove calling from the tall poplar trees.

"Do you remember the nightingale at eventide back at home in Rosenthal?" sighed Tante Anna. "That was the most beautiful sound in the world. Will we ever hear it again?"

Tante Anna's voice trembled. The song of the mourning dove evoked so many memories of a distant homeland. Lisa knew that they grieved for parents and friends banished to Siberia, never to return. She knew that Ma's heart would always remain with the three tiny graves in a faraway cemetery. Sometimes when Ma spoke of the little ones, she seemed to be in a different place in a different time.

As Ma and Tante Anna looked at each other, Lisa saw that they both had tears in their eyes.

Music Lessons

Since Christmas Arn had spent every spare minute with his violin. He could not read music, so Pa helped him work out the basic fingerings and notes from the E-Z violin book. Soon Arn could read and follow the notes instead of playing only by ear.

After chores and supper Arn took a lamp to his room to practice his scales and songs over and over. Ma laughed at the monotonous repetitions, "He sounds like a puppet on a string!"

Some heads in the village were shaking with misgiving!

"No good will come out of this, like as not! That boy has musical talent but this will be the undoing of him, just wait and see. Hasn't he been playing along with the men at Spielstunde? If you are musical you simply play. He should stay with a given gift and not distort it with these quirkings! *Sonderbar,* indeed!"

Arn continued his practicing, totally unaware of these dire predictions. He progressed in reading notes and began to realize how much there was to learn. The E-Z book was not as easy as it proclaimed to be. It was rather vague about shifting positions. He became frustrated and discouraged.

Silently Pa observed his struggles. Something had to be done. But there was no music teacher within a hundred miles.

Meanwhile Arn could play at Spielstunde on a violin

of his very own at last. Many times on Sunday mornings he ran home from the church service in order to play a new hymn on his violin before he could forget it. Sometimes Pa had to tell Arn very firmly that it was time to stop.

One day Pa came home from Winkler with some news. After a discussion with Ma he called Arn into the kitchen.

"Today I heard about a violin teacher who just moved to Winkler. I went to see him to discuss lessons. Since I cannot pay him with money we made a bargain. I offered to bring him a load of hay for his cow in exchange for a few lessons. We will take a load on Saturday and you can stay for your first lesson."

Arn stood there, utterly mute and speechless. The impossible had been made possible! And all by virtue of a cow!

After some moments of stunned silence he ran out and let out a shrill whistle that brought Rover to his side in a flash. Grabbing the dog Arn rolled over and over with him on the grass, as his laughter rang out with relief and joy at the very thought of it! Music lessons! For him!

There was no need for Rover to know about the cow and the hay and the music. With short barks and furious wags of his bushy tail he fully shared his master's moment of joy.

And so, as Arn had his occasional lessons, receiving them as priceless gifts, the cow calmly consumed the hay as her rightful due, all unaware of being instrumental in fulfilling a boy's dream.

There were times when lessons were next to impossible due to rain or sleet. A ride was not always possible so sometimes Arn walked the twelve miles to town. Lessons depended on how long the hay lasted; it was a healthy hungry cow. In the winter months trips to town were often impossible.

Frustration and inspiration were in constant conflict. First of all Arn had to unlearn many undesirable habits that blocked his progress. Because he had

played by ear for so long, Arn had learned inaccuracies in notes and rhythm. His bowing was faulty. Often deeply discouraged, he persisted, patiently spending many hours working on technique. His improvement in sound and intonation became noticeable. Soon he mastered selections like 'Souvenir' and 'Humoresque.'

Although the endless exercises became rather monotonous, Lisa never tired of the violin selections, humming the tunes as she did her homework. Even Ma found herself humming the melody of Minuet in G, as she stirred the endless pots of soup on the kitchen stove. Pa did not hum, but often lowered the pages of the *Bote* he was reading in order to listen.

One day Arn called Lisa to his room. She thought he would play a special piece, but he said, "Lisa, today you will begin to play the violin. This will be your first lesson."

For a moment Lisa was too shocked to speak.

"Oh no, Arn I can't!"

"Of course you can! Why not?"

"But girls don't play the violin. I've never heard of a girl playing the violin. Girls play guitar or piano, but never violin!"

Lisa thought of the young ladies at Spielstunde playing guitars adorned with big red bows.

"Well then, you will be the first!"

Arn always got his way. Lisa learned hesitantly at first, then became more confident as she mastered her first songs, then went on to the Kayser Etudes.

In the village some heads were shaken in concern. A girl playing a violin? Unheard of; surely no good would come of it. This practicing was bad enough for a boy, but for a girl? Certainly her time was better spent doing the useful things of milking, baking and sewing! *Sonderbar! Sonderbar!*

Mrs. Krohn, a firm believer in the sacred work ethic, pronounced the final and ultimate verdict, "She will never get a husband, just you wait and see!"